WOMEN
MAKING A
DIFFERENCE

Compiled by
Peace Mitchell & Katy Garner

Women Changing the World Press acknowledges the Elders and Traditional owners of country throughout Australia and their connection to lands, waters and communities. We pay our respect to Elders past and present and extend that respect to all Aboriginal and Islander peoples today. We honour more than sixty thousand years of Indigenous women's voices, stories, leadership and wisdom.

Copyright © Peace Mitchell and Katy Garner
First published in Australia in 2024
by Women Changing the World Press
an imprint of KMD Books
Waikiki, WA 6169

All rights reserved. No part of this book may be used or reproduced by any means, graphic, electronic or mechanical, including photocopying, recording, taping or by any information storage retrieval system without the written permission of the copyright owner except in the case of brief quotations embodied in critical articles and reviews.

Because of the dynamic nature of the Internet, any web addresses or links contained in this book may have changed since publication and may no longer be valid. The views expressed in this work are solely those of the author and do not necessarily reflect the views of the publisher and the publisher hereby disclaims any responsibility for them.

Edited by Tracy Regan

Typeset in Adobe Garamond Pro 12/17pt

A catalogue record for this work is available from the National Library of Australia

National Library of Australia Catalogue-in-Publication data:
Women Making A Difference/Peace Mitchell and Katy Garner

ISBN:
978-1-7636406-9-6
(Paperback)

To the unsung heroes, the women making a difference all over the world, we see you, we honour you, we thank you. This book is for you.

CONTENTS

INTRODUCTION..ix

BE THE FIRST
Dr Cara Lenore Antoine 5

TRANSFORMATIVE HEALING AND PROACTIVE ADVOCACY
Comfort Dondo 25

THE AFTER IN HAPPILY EVER AFTER
Ellen Hooper 37

A VILLAGE GIRL WITH BIG DREAMS
Florence Kayungwa 51

RECLAIM YOUR SELF-EXPRESSION TO BE YOUR MOST RADIANT SELF
Gaëlle Berruel 63

PAGES OF HOPE
Heather McCarthy 77

WHEN YOUR NAME BECOMES YOUR CALLING
Iris Mhlanga 91

IT IS NEVER TOO LATE
Janette Salmi 103

SUCCESS OR FAILURE?
Justine McLean 117

THE BODACIOUS WOMAN
Kabinga Mazaba 131

BECOMING UNBROKEN
Kate Fisher 147

LESSONS I HAVE LEARNT ALONG THE WAY
Laura Goldberg 161

UNCOMPLICATING EMPATHY
Leanne Butterworth 175

THE ENERGY OF CONSCIOUSNESS
Lisa Benson 189

A LOVE LETTER TO WOMEN IN BUSINESS
Melanie Wentzel 203

LIFE
Nicola Baker 217

BEYOND BAOBABS
Patricia Gonde 229

IDENTITY, MUSIC & SELF-CARE
Rebecca Rylands 245

THE SILENT DIFFERENCE
Dr Sarifa Alonto-Younes 259

EMPOWER TO FEEL EMPOWERED
Zara Celik 271

INTRODUCTION

We're told that making a difference can be as simple as recycling or using a reusable coffee cup, but to truly make a difference in the world and create a lasting impact is often not that simple.

It's true we all can, and should, do our part to make a difference in small ways each day, but for the women who have dedicated their life to a cause, truly making a difference by committing to a higher purpose, it's often not simple at all – in fact, the challenges they face are so great, they sometimes seem impossible.

What does it take to make a difference in our world?

The women featured in this book bravely share their stories of how they are making a difference and what it takes to do this. Rarely is it an easy road. There are challenges each of them have faced along the way, yet the incredible results they've achieved make their struggles worthwhile.

The calling to make a difference is often a strong one. Our mentor, Dr Tererai Trent, asks those longing to find their purpose the question:

'What breaks your heart?'

For many women this question is the key which unlocks the quest to find their calling. There is power and deep healing in supporting others to overcome the heartbreaks we have endured in life.

For so many women, there is deep pain at the heart of their determination to create change; to build a better world for others than the one they were faced with as a child. Turning your pain into purpose is

INTRODUCTION

a powerful and deeply healing way to create change and take back your power and your story.

Your calling is the guiding light you come back to again and again. Through the hard times when it seems time to quit, your calling reminds you of why you are here, why you do this and the vision for the future you want to build. A strong calling is an essential part of the process of change; those who don't feel strongly about why they do what they do probably won't last the distance.

But finding your calling is just the first part in the long process to make a difference in the world.

You must believe it's possible. From a young age, I have always believed that one person has the power to change the world, to make a difference, to create something bigger than themselves, to create a better future for others. So, you can imagine my surprise when I realised that not everyone thinks like that. The first time someone said to me, 'You can't change the world, you know,' was a shock to me. I had always believed this to be fundamentally true. But not everyone is raised as I was. My mindset and belief is that not only can you change the world, but you should do your part to make a difference. I've discovered this isn't a common belief, and if you don't believe it's possible to make a difference, then creating change will be a lot harder.

Having a calling and the belief that it is possible is essential, but you will also need commitment, dedication, determination, persistence and resilience. You need a stubbornness that stops you from quitting when everyone around you is telling you that you should, the grit to do the hard work when needed and the positivity to celebrate every little win and tiny glimmer of success along the way.

These are the stories you'll hear about in these pages; real women sharing real stories of dedication, determination and persistence – no matter what. The commitment to making a difference and the years of work it takes to get there. The inspired action combined with the courage to try again until you succeed.

Making a difference is often long, slow, hard work over many years. It is not easy or glamorous. There will be setbacks and hurdles, sometimes too many. It will break your heart all over again, but the indescribable feeling of knowing that you have genuinely been a part of something meaningful makes all the struggles and challenges worthwhile.

This is why we do what we do, and this is why we encourage you to follow your calling and make a difference too.

Peace Mitchell

BE THE FIRST

Dr Cara Lenore Antoine

INTRODUCTION

Picture a pivotal moment in my teenage years, where, at fourteen, I became the first girl in my school to delve into electrical engineering. While it was daunting, I was confident, thanks to the conviction of my teacher who said: 'I believe in you.' I now felt I could achieve anything I set my mind to.

In the intricate tapestry of human experience, stories play a key role. As we navigate a world dictated by conformity, being 'the first' represents a beacon of courage, innovation and transformative change.

In this chapter, I want to take you through my narrative and those of others who dared to be pioneers, making a major impact on society, the planet and the greater collective good.

Consider compelling figures in the early 1960s, such as Katherine Johnson, Dorothy Vaughan and Mary Jackson, who shattered racial and gender barriers at NASA. Being 'the first' for them involved dismantling discrimination, shaping space science and paving the way for inclusivity.

Why is this relevant today? It encapsulates the excitement of driving innovation, breaking down longstanding barriers and assuming a leadership role. It involves a sense of responsibility – representing and advocating for the under-represented while influencing positive change.

Throughout this chapter, I highlight diverse examples of women who have made a significant impact in areas ranging from space exploration and technology to environmental activism, politics, science, innovation, business, sustainability, athletics and animal welfare. They have broken barriers to pave the way for greater diversity and inclusivity in these fields and society as a whole, and they serve as inspirations for future generations.

So, let the stories unfold. Welcome to a journey where each step paves the way for a future defined by innovation, inclusivity and enduring impact.

INDRA NOOYI
As the first woman and person of colour to lead PepsiCo as its CEO, she broke barriers in the corporate world and advocated for sustainability and diversity in business.

KATHERINE JOHNSON
As a NASA mathematician, Katherine calculated the trajectories for the first American spaceflights, including the first moon landing.

KATHRYN BIGELOW
The first woman to win the Academy Award for Best Director for her work on the film *The Hurt Locker*. Her win brought attention to gender disparities in the film industry.

HEDY LAMARR
She was an actress and inventor who co-invented frequency hopping, which is the basis for modern wireless communication.

SIMONE BILES
As a highly accomplished gymnast, Simone Biles has broken multiple records and is often considered one of the greatest gymnasts of all time. She has been 'the first' in many gymnastics achievements and has inspired countless young athletes.

WOMEN MAKING A DIFFERENCE

BREAKING BARRIERS

Does 'one size fit all'? Not in my experience. During my years of working at a global energy company, I wore a lot of personal protection equipment (PPE) at our sites and facilities. Most sites did not have gear for women, so we wore men's protective clothing.

Depending on the region I was in, for much of Europe and the USA, I wore extra-small and in Asia, extra-large! The steel-tipped safety boots were often oversized, and I never enjoyed putting my feet into someone else's sweaty shoes. The front trouser zipper on the jumpsuit coveralls served no purpose for us women, and the gloves that were made for men were typically coated in grease and grime.

On assignment at one facility, where there were only two other women on an over four-hundred-person manned site, I was able to be a catalyst for change. The other women and I decided to get together to be the first to develop new PPE – designed by women, for women.

The catalyst for becoming the first often lies in recognising a critical need for change or improvement. It's not merely about seeing something that needs to be done differently; it's about feeling a responsibility to make things better for everyone involved.

One immediate benefit was that we could keep our own PPE rather than suiting up in someone else's gear. And the longer-term effect – once we started to make women's PPE available for women at all our global sites, was that we collectively felt as though we belonged at the company. That was so empowering. Knowing how important it was to other women made a huge difference for us all.

Breaking barriers is not just about statistics or organisational benefits; it's about individuals who choose to be the torchbearers of change. By breaking the mould, they introduce a fresh perspective, paving the way for a more innovative and inclusive future; a cornerstone for achieving substantial impact in the workplace and the communities we inhabit. In professional spheres, particularly in business and technology, women breaking through barriers is akin to opening the floodgates of innovation. It's not merely a triumph for the individual; it's an affirmation that diversity is needed for progress.

Why is this theme critical? Being the first to break barriers matters because it reshapes the narrative, injecting diversity and inclusion into the DNA of industries. It's about shattering preconceived notions, challenging stereotypes and carving a path for future generations. When women step into roles traditionally dominated by men, it sends a powerful message – a message that diversity is not just a buzzword but a key to unlocking untapped potential.

Imagine the ripple effect. As actor Victor Webster said, 'Everything we do, even the slightest thing we do, can have a ripple effect … If you throw a pebble into the water on one side of the ocean, it can create a tidal wave on the other side.' I consider each of the actions I take as my pebbles. Working with others, I believe we can create the ripples that will cause a tidal wave of change. As women carve their paths, they reverberate through communities, inspiring others to dream bigger, aim higher and embrace opportunities beyond societal expectations. Breaking barriers is both a personal journey and a commitment to fostering an environment where everyone, regardless of gender, can thrive and contribute.

So, consider breaking barriers a call to action, a pledge to champion diversity and inclusion, and a road map for future generations to follow. It's not merely about being the first; it's also about encouraging others to embrace their unique strengths, challenge the status quo and actively contribute to a landscape where diversity is not just celebrated but recognised as a driving force for transformative innovation. It lays the foundation for a future where barriers are dismantled and success knows no gender.

WOMEN MAKING A DIFFERENCE

ROSA PARKS
Often called 'The First Lady of Civil Rights', her refusal to give up her bus seat in Montgomery, Alabama, in 1955 was a pivotal moment in the civil rights movement, challenging racial segregation.

KAMALA HARRIS
In 2021, Kamala Harris became the first woman, first Black woman and first person of South Asian descent to be elected vice president of the United States. Her historic election shattered multiple barriers in politics.

GITANJALI RAO
In 2020, at the age of fifteen, Gitanjali Rao was named the first-ever *Time* Magazine Kid of the Year for her innovative work in science and technology, particularly for her inventions in water quality testing and preventing cyberbullying.

KATIE SOWERS
In 2020, Katie Sowers became the first openly gay coach in the NFL, working as an offensive assistant with the San Francisco 49ers. Her role has contributed to increased LGBTQ+ representation in professional sports.

KOBKARN WATTANAVRANGKUL
Kobkarn was the first female Minister of Tourism and Sports in Thailand, serving from 2014 to 2017. Her leadership promoted tourism and cultural exchange in the country.

DR CARA LENORE ANTOINE

PIONEERING REPRESENTATION

Being the first isn't a solo act; it's a collaborative effort, a shared belief in untapped potential and a journey that goes beyond individual accolades.

As a young girl, I fell in love with tech and science. My early inspiration came from reading the stories and accomplishments of great pioneers like Grace Hopper, Jane Goodall and Amelia Earhart. When I signed up for electrical engineering (EE) at fourteen, I was the only girl in the class. My teacher taught me how to build a radio. I quickly learned how to solder different coloured wires, secure them to a circuit board, attach a speaker and create a sound. And I was hooked!

Ever since my teacher empowered me with their belief in me, I have sought ways to tell women that I believe in them. To achieve equality in the tech workforce by 2030, another five million girls and women will need to choose a career in technology.

Picture this: today, forty years after stepping into that EE class as a young girl, I proudly hold the title of 'the first' female chief technology and innovation officer (CTIO) at my company. My manager, another trailblazer, made the bold decision to hire a female CTIO. Throughout my career, I've often been a lone woman in business and tech environments, breaking new ground. This requires a blend of vision, determination and a passion for positive change, creating opportunities for others and shattering ceilings.

The achievement of being the first can serve as a source of inspiration for others and create new opportunities. It provides a role model for others, showing that it's possible to overcome challenges and succeed.

Women must step into uncharted territory, push boundaries and be pioneers. I invite you to be inspired, to step out of your comfort zones, try new things and become pioneers in your own right, whether advocating for yourself or others, exploring non-traditional career paths or pursuing long-held dreams.

Imagine a world where women holding leadership roles advocate for policies and changes that benefit everyone. It's not a utopia; it's a vision we can collectively work towards. This theme is a call to action, compelling us to champion leadership and representation for women, whether through supporting them in leadership roles, encouraging political participation or advocating for diverse representation in all spheres of society.

Representation matters. Being the first provides representation for under-represented groups. Seeing someone who looks like them or shares similar experiences can inspire individuals who might not have considered pursuing those opportunities.

So, remember your role – be a supporter and advocate for women in leadership roles and act, contributing to a more equitable and sustainable world.

RITU KARIDHAL
In 2019, Ritu Karidhal was the deputy operations director for India's Mars Orbiter Mission (Mangalyaan), making her a prominent woman scientist in India and a pioneering figure in the Indian space program.

SANNA MARIN
In 2019, at the age of thirty-four, Sanna Marin became the youngest prime minister of Finland and the world's youngest serving state leader. She also led a coalition government dominated by women.

MAE JEMISON
In 1992, Mae Jemison became the first African-American woman to travel to space as a NASA astronaut. She's also a physician and engineer, advocating for diversity in STEM fields.

SHERRI FRANKLIN
Sherri Franklin is the founder of Muttville, a non-profit organisation dedicated to senior dog rescue. She has been a driving force in the animal rescue world, advocating for the adoption of older dogs.

ARLAN HAMILTON
Arlan Hamilton is the founder of Backstage Capital, a venture capital fund dedicated to investing in under-represented founders in tech. She is the first Black woman to start a venture capital fund in the United States.

WOMEN MAKING A DIFFERENCE

EMPOWERING THROUGH EDUCATION AND MENTORSHIP

Exploring this theme highlights the indispensable role of education and mentorship.

Empowering communities: digital literacy as a gateway

As the chair for digital literacy at the G100, I aim to empower communities through digital skills. This role has enabled me to provide a gateway for others to thrive in the digital age, annually upskilling one hundred women in digital literacy. In parallel, organisations have become more inclusive, recognising the value of diversity in contributing to success and progress. By actively encouraging more girls to embrace coding, I am contributing to breaking down stereotypes and creating tangible pathways for the next generation.

Global collaboration: education as a catalyst for change

Beyond borders, my collaboration with the International Chambers of Commerce and global communities aims to bring education and tech skills to underprivileged locations, such as to girls and women in Afghanistan. I love knowing that the digital skills these girls are getting can help them start careers as freelancers in tech. When it comes to efforts closer to home, I visit classrooms around the Netherlands to enable young students in underprivileged districts with digital literacy upskilling such as low-code programming and how to build a robot. The impact of these programs isn't just measured in statistics; it's about the lives transformed, the opportunities created and the empowerment of individuals who were once overlooked. This is the power of leveraging influence for meaningful global change.

The transformative power of education

Education is a transformative force that can reshape destinies. As individuals break barriers to become the first in their fields, access to quality education becomes the catalyst for greater opportunities. This mindset has motivated me to create opportunities for advanced degree scholarships in partnership with tech institutions and universities, such as MSM and MBA programs in data science, data analytics and digital transformation. Staying longer in school opens doors to a multitude of possibilities, empowering women to rise not only in their careers, but in every facet of their lives.

I envision a world where education is a universal right, where every girl has the chance to step into the realm of knowledge.

Mentorship as the guiding light
Mentorship takes centrestage as the guiding light that illuminates the path forward. As individuals break barriers, mentorship becomes a crucial element in navigating the complexities of their careers. Experienced leaders serve as beacons, offering insights and the tools necessary to overcome challenges. In this light, I have developed an annual series of role model masterclasses for women in tech, a youth ambassador program, as well as offering early career mentoring.

Mentorship is not merely a personal benefit; it becomes a force that propels change on a broader scale. Women, as the first in their fields, evolve into advocates for diversity and inclusion through mentorship. Their rise creates a positive cycle of empowerment, where every step forward lifts others, fostering a community that thrives on shared knowledge and support.

Creating opportunities for all
Education and mentorship intertwine to create a tapestry of opportunities. Being the first not only opens doors for trailblazers but also sets the stage for mentorship, networking and support systems to flourish. These opportunities are the orchestrators of a more inclusive and diverse

professional landscape. As women rise through education and mentorship, they become living testaments to the possibilities that lie ahead.

I invite you to join this storyline of empowerment. Support educational initiatives and mentorship programs for women and girls. Be the guiding star and role model for those who have yet to find their way in this enriching journey of life.

DR FEI-FEI LI
Dr Fei-Fei Li is a computer scientist and the first female director of the Stanford Artificial Intelligence Lab. She's the 'godmother of AI' – a pioneer in the field of artificial intelligence and computer vision.

HINDOU OUMAROU IBRAHIM
Hindou Oumarou Ibrahim is an environmental activist from Chad and one of the first Indigenous women to be appointed as a United Nations Sustainable Development Goal Advocate. She advocates for climate action and the rights of Indigenous peoples.

LYNN CONWAY
Lynn Conway is a pioneer in the field of microelectronics and computer science. She made groundbreaking contributions to chip design methodology and is known for her role in the VLSI (very large-scale integration) revolution.

AYUMI MOORE AOKI
As the founder and CEO of Women in Tech Global, a non-profit organisation that aims to close the gender gap in the science, technology, engineering, arts and mathematics (STEAM) fields, she's a leading advocate to empower five million women and girls in STEAM by 2030.

WANGARI MAATHAI
Wangari Maathai was the first African woman to win the Nobel Peace Prize in 2004. She was recognised for her environmental and political activism, particularly her efforts in tree planting and women's rights through the Green Belt Movement.

WOMEN MAKING A DIFFERENCE

REFLECTION

Embarking on this empowering journey, we explore narratives shaping change. I encourage you to hold an unwavering belief that turns challenges into opportunities and has the immense potential to be a catalyst for institutional change. Embrace the journey collaboratively; being the first is about recognising potential together.

Innovation thrives in diverse landscapes, enriching individuals and organisations. I invite you to embrace the power of diversity by driving change and equality in the world, while preserving human values. The journey doesn't end by being the first; it continues collaboratively, progressing to a future that celebrates diversity.

This is your profound call to action:

1. Challenge stereotypes: Actively dismantle gender-based stereotypes for unhindered pursuit of passions.
2. Promote inclusivity: Support diversity in workplaces and relationships; champion inclusive organisations.
3. Empower through education: Advocate for quality education and mentorship, recognising their transformative impact.
4. Be THE change-maker: Take tangible actions and engage in initiatives fostering inclusivity and valuing diversity.
5. Champion leadership and representation: Encourage women's leadership, advocating diverse representation.

Transformative change is within your grasp, and you can contribute to a world where women shape a better future for themselves and the collective good. Your actions can represent a ripple effect that goes beyond individual success to become part of a collective force for change.

As you navigate your own journey, I encourage you to draw inspiration from this narrative and recognise that, like me, you too can be a change-maker, positively influencing the world around you. I want you to be the first. The script is yours; step into the limelight and be part of this journey toward a brighter, more inclusive future. Ensure that the path is not isolated and empower others to maximise their success.

As Viola Davis put it, 'To move through life with any level of grace and break generational curses, you have to be a hero.' Embrace your heroism, define where your life goes and be brave in shaping a destiny that transcends generations.

And remember, *I believe in you.*

DR CARA LENORE ANTOINE

Dr Cara Lenore Antoine is a renowned global leader and innovative speaker who is passionate about creating positive change in society, the economy and our planet. A technology advocate, education champion and empowering executive, Dr Antoine enables people and organisations to achieve their full potential in the digital era. With three decades of dedicated experience, Dr Antoine is a powerful agent of growth and transformation, driving impact at the intersection of technology and humanity.

As the Executive Vice President and Chief Technology, Innovation and Portfolio Officer of Capgemini Europe, Dr Antoine strategically advises global corporations in the C-suite across industries on applying innovation to drive and accelerate digital and cultural transformation. With a strong background in digital technology, innovation, B2B and B2C operations, digital marketing and sustainability, she has flourished at some of the world's most prestigious companies, including Microsoft, Royal Shell, Hewlett-Packard, Compaq and Polaroid.

A beacon of excellence in the industry, she has been honoured with recent accolades such as Women Changing the World's 2023 'Global Leader of the Year Award' and the 'Top Woman in Corporate Award', Women in Governance, Risk and Compliance's 2023 'Environmental, Social and Governance (ESG) Officer of the Year Award', Global Women in Tech's 2022 'Global Excellence Award', Computable's 2021 'Top 100 Most Influential Women In Business' and multiple Digital Leader of the Year titles, as well as being named Global Digital Female Leader at the Global Digital Women's Conference in 2022.

DR CARA LENORE ANTOINE

Leveraging her success to help future generations break down barriers to creating a better future in tech-focused fields, she serves on several boards. As a patient leader, Dr Antoine is a catalyst for digitalising visual health and this led her to join the board as awards chairwoman at the Cornea Patient Association, to serve on the advisory board of Easee (the first CE and FDA-certified online eye-exam), and as transformation leader at the Digital Health Committee and Registries of the European Society for Cataract and Refractive Surgeons. She is the chair for Digital Literacy at the G100 and the chairwoman at Women In Tech Netherlands, where she is a fierce advocate and pioneer dedicated to promoting diversity and equity while empowering women within science, technology, engineering, the arts and mathematics (STEAM) worldwide.

TRANSFORMATIVE HEALING AND PROACTIVE ADVOCACY

A JOURNEY OF RESILIENCE

Comfort Dondo

2015-2017: DROWNING TO STANDING - A PERSONAL AND COMMUNITY EVOLUTION

The Weight of the World: Navigating Demands and Expectations

When it comes to changing the world, I decided to write this chapter in the brightest light to shine a spotlight on some of the challenges 'world change-makers' may face, but may not always share. While we receive accolades and even acknowledgements at times, world change-makers like me, working in a field centred around trauma and personal experiences, must first learn the importance of healing the healer first, before pouring from an empty place.

Changing my story, community and world.

During the tumultuous years between 2015 and 2017, my life resembled a stormy sea, navigating homelessness, escaping domestic abuse, and striving to protect my three children. Fuelled by a desperate need for change, I embarked on a mission to not only find solutions for my own plight, but to extend a lifeline to my community. This period marked the genesis of my involvement with survivors of gender-based violence, human trafficking and sexual violence from the African diaspora.

The birthing of the first refuge, which had initially been my own sanctuary, became a symbol of hope for fellow survivors. As I immersed myself in crisis intervention work, I began to sense a shift within me – a realisation that transcended the immediate need for survival. The imperative to transform from merely treading water to standing on solid ground began to take root. In establishing this 'safe haven for other women', I later realised I was trying to continue to offer a lifeline for other women, while my own was still shaky. Hence the realisation that I needed to slow down and reflect on how much capacity I had to serve others.

2020-2022: NAVIGATING THE PANDEMIC – CHALLENGES AND EXPANSION

The onset of the COVID-19 pandemic in 2020 presented both unprecedented challenges and unexpected opportunities for expansion. Amidst the chaos of Minneapolis' homeless encampments, exacerbated by the murder of George Floyd and ensuing uprisings, my advocacy work faced its greatest trial.

As a defender of justice and a comforter of my community, the pandemic forced me to reflect on my own trajectory. It became clear that my personal mission and vision needed a profound recalibration. The struggle against crisis and injustice propelled me towards a deeper understanding of the transformative potential of proactive healing work for myself, and cultivating more rest, joy and healing in myself, so I could offer it for those I work with and lead.

2022: The Gift of Clarity and Leadership Fellowship

The year 2022 unfolded as a precious gift, bringing new-found clarity to my vision and personal mission. Winning the esteemed Bush Fellowship[1] marked a pivotal moment, not only supporting my personal healing but also nurturing my growth as a leader. In my second year as a Bush Fellow, the journey of rediscovery and relearning how to lead took centrestage. Spending a whole year investing in time and space to create rest, joy and restoring time lost from when I immigrated to the United States, I managed to rest for the first time in nineteen years. I had the privilege to cultivate joy, rest, healing and expansion.

---

1 https://www.bushfoundation.org/news/congratulations-2022-bush-fellows#:~:text=The%20Fellowship%20is%20open%20to,that%20share%20the%20same%20geography.

KEY TAKEAWAYS FOR TRANSFORMATIVE HEALING AND PROACTIVE ADVOCACY

- Love and Light: Embrace the present, loving both the place you are at and yourself fully, illuminating the cracks that still need healing.
- Prioritise Your Healing: Be present in your healing journey, recognising the importance of placing yourself at the top of the priority list – akin to the airplane safety analogy of securing your oxygen mask before assisting others.
- Seasonal Awareness: Acknowledge the seasons in your journey – personal, professional and spiritual. Recognise when the season for crisis intervention is over, and proactively transition to the next phase.
- Regular Inventory Checks: Perform regular inventory checks in your space – personally and professionally. Adapt, change and improve to enhance impact without succumbing to stagnancy.
- Healed Healer: Acknowledge that after life experiences, the healer must actively engage in their own healing journey. Recognise the impacts of secondary trauma and burnout, prioritising rest to remain impactful and present in your advocacy work.
- As the healer becomes more healed, the transformative impact ripples outward, shaping a legacy of resilience and empowerment. The metamorphosis from crisis intervention to proactive healing is not just an individual evolution, it's a communal awakening. The healer, now fortified with a deeper understanding of their own journey, becomes a catalyst for change within their community.

COMFORT DONDO

Phumulani Minnesota African Women against Violence – Women at the Well Project, Founding Executive Director
Alkubelin Wellness Collective, CEO president: A coalition of African diaspora community leaders and research consulting firm, bridging the gap between government agencies and grassroot organisations.

PROFESSIONAL EXPERIENCE

- Founder | Phumulani Minnesota African Women Against Violence | February 2015 – Present.
- Founded and established the first African Immigrant women's emergency shelter in Minnesota, raising over $500K in the first two years of inception.
- Directs, leads, and mentors a team of seventeen, establishing KPIs in alignment with company vision and goals.
- Creates and builds collaborative partnerships with 92+ community-based agencies to reduce violence against women within Minnesota communities.
- Develops and writes grant proposals ranging from $10,000 to $1 Million, increasing the portfolio over a million dollars.
- Serves as subject matter expert, sitting on the Governor's Taskforce, providing guidance and advice to the office of the Governor on the needs of historically marginalised communities improving policies to become more family and community centred.
- Identifies needs, directing community building efforts to transform outreach initiatives for fostering meaningful partnerships and

promoting family wellbeing.
- Develops and implements marketing initiatives resulting in building effective community partnerships.
- Designs and implements programs to drive communication among members, creating community and belonging, while addressing risks and needs.
- Identifies fundraising opportunities, raising and disbursing $1 million to Black-Led Change after George Floyd's ,urder
- Led Healing Circles following the George Floyd protests.
- Oversees community housing needs in times of crisis, housing 300+ survivors of sexual violence and homelessness during the peak of Covid-19.
- Collaborates with analysing strategies and donor possibilities to cultivate individual gifts from corporate partner executives resulting in increased philanthropic contributions, strengthened partnerships, and enhanced support for our mission and initiatives.
- Engages board members and key stakeholders in donor visits, improving donor relationships, fostering a deeper understanding of our organization's impact, and ultimately increasing financial support for our mission and programs.
- Plans, manages, and executes initiatives in support of strategic planning, prospecting, and developing complex investment opportunities, and grant management, improving organisational sustainability, fostering innovation, and enhancing the overall effectiveness of our mission-driven programs.

AWARDS
- Miss Africa Minnesota 2006.
- Gary M. DeCramer Leadership Award at the Humphrey School of Public Affairs 2018.
- Global Woman Award in the "Survivor Activist" Global Women

Foundation Washington University .
- Brooklyn Park Mayor's Awardee 'Connecting Community Advocacy Award'.
- Violence Free Minnesota 2021 Advocate of the Year Award
- Bush Fellowship Awardee 2022.
- Black Foundation Community Builder Winner (One of the fifteen chosen grant makers).
- St Catherine University 2021 Alumni of the Year Award 2021.
- Humanitarian Impact in the Women Changing the World Award Dr Trent Nominated (Oprah Winfrey's favorite guest).
- 2023 National Philanthropy Award Day Awardee 'Providing Safety for Immigrant Survivors'.

EDUCATION & CERTIFICATIONS
- Master's Public Affairs Policy Phi Alpha Honors.
- University of Minnesota Humphrey School of Public Affairs.
- United Nations Scholar.

THE AFTER IN HAPPILY EVER AFTER

Ellen Hooper

Someone wise once told me that the equation for happiness is *expectation minus reality*.

When it comes to the egg-and-spoon race of balancing parenting, a loving partnership and a meaningful career, the gap between what we expect and what we experience can be vast.

The stats are stacked up against us – high rates of divorce, parental burnout and mental illness. Yet, so many of us are ready to roll the dice and think that for us, it will be different.

And who can blame us? Almost every fairytale and romantic comedy ends at the point in time where, for most of us, the real work starts.

The idea that 'true love's kiss' is the conclusion of a story rather than the beginning of one hasn't set us up particularly well for the real world. In 1993, D:Ream released the classic hit, 'Things Can Only Get Better' and declared that things could only get better *now I've found you*. Clearly those guys hadn't had kids yet.

For most people, our love stories are the prologue to a manual we quickly realise we need – how to make the mundane cogs in the wheel of day-to-day life fit together.

For those of us who couple up and have kids, life has offered up a riddle that not many of us have solved. How do you maintain two healthy, happy adults without subtracting from a healthy, happy kid(s)?

Having grown up in a Spice-Girls-infused era of 'girl power', my expectations were very clear. I was told I could be anything I wanted to be … and I was going to have it all.

I was on a mission: to unlock the secret code to having a marriage that didn't drive me nuts, children that I actually liked, and a career that others would consider successful. I was searching for answers.

When Sheryl Sandberg's book *Lean In* came out, I couldn't wait to read it. I hoped that it held in it the answers for how a young lady, full of ambition, was meant to deal with the inequality she had been vaguely assured was part of the history books, and therefore, not a reality she had prepared for.

Lean In has a range of advice for working women, some of which has stood the test of time and some that hasn't. But one piece of advice she gave fuelled me forward: *The most important career choice you'll make is who you marry.*

Armed with this information, at the ripe age of twenty-five, I knew what I had to do. I set forth to interrogate my husband.

We were newly married and on holiday in Tasmania. It was cold. We were driving up a windy road to get to the top of some mountain. The topic of conversation – *should we have a baby?*

On the question of procreation, I was open to being convinced, but I wanted to know how the logistics would work. Would we truly be in this together? Would it be a true partnership? I was on guard for being hoodwinked into a life of servitude that would see me lose myself and all I had worked for. 'Could we please not be like the other parents?' I asked, the idea that we had some special skill being the lie that every parent tells themselves before the sausage factory of life spits you out into the exact same casing that everyone else is trapped in.

As predicted, the discussion turned to work. How would work, *work?* What time would he be willing to take off? What would my body, my baby and my sanity cope with?

I remember as our car crawled up the mountain, the tension inside the car also rose. 'How much time do I have to take off?' he said, exasperated with my naive persistence for specifics, certainty and fairness. It wasn't exactly yelling. It was yelling adjacent.

'Well, how much time do *I* have to take off?' I was definitely yelling.

As you would expect from two legally trained, relentlessly stubborn high-achievers, the negotiations were long and comprehensive. Talking to other parents now, it turns out that this type of discussion and particularly the detail of it, is quite unusual.

After many amendments, addendums and blood oaths, we did decide to give the baby thing a crack. Unsurprisingly, despite the best-laid plans, the real work lay ahead of us.

Apparently, it takes ten thousand hours to master a skill.

When my son was born, I had literally never changed a nappy. My husband had taken six weeks off work, and during that, we spent time together working this little creature out. What did he need? How did it work? What was normal and what wasn't? How were we meant to sleep?

At that stage, much of my career has been about adult learning and development, and by work standards, we were graduate level. Not particularly fast nor particularly competent, but we were doing okay for our expected skill level.

When that six weeks ended and Matt put his suit back on, something happened. The baby kept changing, and because I was putting in all the hours, I was changing too. I was learning. I was becoming an expert. After his first week back at work, Friday night came, and we were relieved.

My husband took the baby. I was thrilled. We were watching TV. The baby was crying. My husband put the baby in the crook between his folded knees and gave his legs a little jiggle. A technique he had developed a week and a half ago.

What a great idea, we had congratulated ourselves then. How cute! How clever we were.

But now. The baby was still crying. Now, literally five days later, he was doing it wrong. The knee jiggle wouldn't cut it anymore. The baby liked rocking now. It was crazy and idiotic for him to think that knee jiggling would work.

And that's all it took. Five days. Five days of him at work and me at home. Five days of constant change and minimal sleep. 120 hours. 120 hours was what it took for my husband to become an idiot. The expectation I had about our equal parenting was high, but the practical realities of life were falling short.

Is there a reason that parents, despite their best intentions, fall into the same trap over and over again?

Many of you will think that the reason is biological. Women are nurturing. Men are wired to want to provide. Hunters and gathers. Men are from Mars, while women are from Venus.

We're learning more and more that this isn't the case. Gina Rippon, a British professor of cognitive neuroimaging, dedicates an entire book, *Gender and Our Brains* (2019), to the question of whether men and women have different brains. Gina's thesis is that, since we know the brain is malleable or plastic and it's capable of growing and changing, we'll never be truly able to know what's gender-based and what is the impact of how we treat our children (particularly based on their gender), and how their tiny plastic-y brains change in response.

But here's where the hunter/gather idea starts to lose traction. While scientists have studied oxytocin (known as the 'love hormone') levels in mothers for a long time now, about ten years ago, (along with colleagues) Dr Ruth Feldman, from the Centre for Developmental Social Neuroscience, found that fathers who interact with their newborns have identical levels of oxytocin to new mums (Gordon et al, 2010).

She also went on to study male gay couples who were the primary carers of their children since birth and found that men who were the primary caregivers have the same activation in the amygdala part of their brain as new mothers do (Abraham et al, 2014).

Isn't that incredible? Basically, if you choose to be the committed caregiver, regardless of your gender or biological relationship with the child, biology doesn't hold you back – it says 'cool, we're here for it'.

The challenge is that it's not easy to rewrite the rules of our cultural norms.

Social change is more abstract art than paint by number. When we look back through history, the changes that have been successful have had a mix of individual and 'collective' actions. The personal is the political, as they say.

When it comes to redefining the way we structure our parenting partnerships (whether we're in a romantic relationship or not), I don't want to pretend that sitting down and dividing your household tasks is going to magically overthrow the patriarchy.

I do know that if every single parent in your country did so, a monumental, collective shift would surely take place.

I also know there are lots of laws in place across the globe to prevent discrimination and 'ensure' equality. Yet, we still have gender pay gaps in almost every country. I also know that people are disproportionately subjected to violence at the hands of men, and that men are more likely to kill themselves. Laws aren't enough either.

Change happens slowly, with multiple layers stitching together.

I don't make laws, or run a big company, so I focus on what I know and on what individuals can do to change the dynamics between parents, so that everyone's left holding the baby *equally*.

In many ways, the dilemma that faces us is a battle for a finite resource – time.

As we add kids into the mix, we start getting pulled in different directions, trying to find time for:

- Our children and their needs.
- Our work – our ability to be financially secure and (hopefully) make a purposeful contribution.
- Ourselves – our physical, mental, emotional and (perhaps) spiritual wellbeing.
- Our relationships (sometimes but not always marriage) and our

friendships.
- The day-to-day logistics of life (keeping the 'house' going).

Honestly, it's hard. While the way that women have entered the workplace has changed dramatically over the last fifty years, the way that men engage with kids and 'home' is changing more slowly.

Here is what my career in helping adults learn how to develop new skills has taught me – the skills we need for parenting, marriage, leadership and work are all the same. They are the skills of human connection.

They're the skills we should put our focus on, so that we can make deliberate choices about what we spend our time on as a team, rather than fight each other for it.

One of the best things we can do is let each other learn. The parent who puts in the initial time 'in the trenches' (usually a woman) learns first. They get the PhD in the baby. The hardest thing to do when you have developed incredible expertise is to watch someone else, someone who's barely got a high school certificate in the baby, to start to learn.

Adults learn by doing. When we learn something new, we all start at zero. The more ferociously we guard our expertise, the bigger that capability gap is and the more alone we are.

My husband took parental leave when our eldest was nine months old and I went back to work full-time. We had an explicit discussion – he was in charge; he wanted to do it his way. He didn't want to be nagged by me. I didn't want to be a nag.

On the first weekend, we were getting ready to go to a friend's house for lunch. As the baby was (finally) dressed and placed in his car seat, I realised something; he didn't have the baby bag – the one with wipes and spare clothes and most importantly – diapers.

I froze in indecision. I could gently remind him about the bag, likely causing nagging-related fury. I could get the bag, likely making the bag my sole responsibility for eternity. Or I could quietly get in the car and chalk it up to a learning experience.

When we got to our friend's house, I stayed as far away from that baby as possible. Finally, the moment arrived. 'Where's the baby bag?' he asked. I didn't have it. And guess what? He had a problem to solve, and he solved it. He found another parent with a baby, borrowed a diaper (well, I hope we didn't return it) and all was well.

Here's the thing. I have forgotten to take some essential child item with me many times. It's not that I am a perfect parent, and neither is my husband. It's that we both need opportunities to learn, and we learn best through experiences. Now we've both handled a baby without a spare diaper, we're both better at bringing one (or two, in case someone else forgets theirs). And most importantly, that's a responsibility that lives in both of our brains, not just mine.

It's taken us many years of intense work to mould our parenting partnership in the way we want to. While we are nowhere near perfect, we are improving.

Recently, my husband came back from a trip to the dentist with our kid. Three fillings were needed. 'I probably should have gone every six months like they recommended instead of waiting eighteen months,' he lamented, simultaneously regretful and sheepish.

There would have been times earlier in parenting where I would have been flooded with guilt, in some pretend alternate universe where I should be responsible for everything child related. And an even more unrealistic idea, that if I was, I would never make a mistake.

There also would have been times when I would have been mad.

After lots of practice, we give each other more compassion. I know he's got this, that he'll take on the consequences of a missed dentist appointment – he ended up having to take our kid to the dentist four times over twelve weeks, so now he's fastidious about their appointments.

In return, I (mostly) receive the same grace when I lose my temper with a child or forget that it's pyjama day at day care.

When we're in a system that is designed for us to fail, it's easy to turn against each other. So often, discussions of gender are framed as *men versus women*. From the many discussions I've had with parents, mostly we're looking to have the contributions we make acknowledged and the struggles we experience understood.

What a difference it would make if it was you and me, united against this deeply flawed system that's out to undermine, instead of you and me against each other.

Someone wise also once told me that we can do anything, but we definitely can't do everything. Maybe we should stop trying to have it all and start being clear about what is truly important to us, as individuals, as partners and as a family. I know that things really do get better if we do them together.

ELLEN HOOPER

Ellen Hooper is a people and culture expert and an award-winning coach and people leader. She's a certified coach with the International Coaching Federation, an accredited mediator, a passionate speaker and loves to help individuals and groups to grow and develop.

Her clients call her a coaching magician and a total legend who helps them get unstuck and she has been described by the Australian of the Year 2023 as her 'secret weapon'.

Ellen was named as a finalist in the 2023 Stevie International Women in Business Awards for Social Change Maker of the Year – Gender and a winner in the 2023 Australia-wide AusMumpreneur Awards for Coach of the Year (Silver) and Leadership Excellence (Bronze).

Ellen started her career as an employment lawyer and worked her way up to being a people and culture C-suite executive. She is now a non-executive director, co-founder of a leadership development company (the Growth Collective), keynote speaker, writer and career and retirement coach.

A VILLAGE GIRL WITH BIG DREAMS

Florence Kayungwa

Life can be difficult to comprehend. Indeed, there is no definite formula anyone can follow to archive greatness, but a wise man once said that *some people are like seeds sown by the farmer; wherever they fall, they always find a way to germinate.*

I was born into a family of two, in a small village called Makande in Hurungwe, Zimbabwe. When a child is born, people usually celebrate the birth of a new life in their family, but in my case, it was the other way round. Instead of my mother and father celebrating, my father wasn't happy because I am a girl. In my paternal family, they believe that giving birth to a girl child is a punishment from the Gods. In some African families, they still cling to their belief that the birth of a girl child is *worthless*, even though the world is civilised, with the feminist movement now common in every part of the world and women taking the driver's seat in all areas of life.

My mother gave birth to another girl after three years, which led to her divorce because my father and his family wanted a boy. We moved to my maternal grandmother's home and lived with them. My grandmother explained to me from that early age, that my own father didn't like me because I was a girl, but her best advice was, 'Keep that in mind and prove them wrong.' She would tell me folk tales where a woman was always the hero – though that did sometimes irk me.

Growing up, I was, and still am, fascinated by high-heeled stiletto shoes. Whenever I see someone wearing high-heeled shoes I associate them with greatness. I picture myself in those empowering shoes, with my chest out, walking with confidence because I know who I am. I used to stare at my grade two teacher's shoes to such an extent that she noticed.

Mrs Magondo once told me they were shoes for the learned. I vividly remember her saying, 'These shoes symbolise freedom. They remind you that you are in control of everything. Imagine walking around in this point shoe …' When playing with other children I would imitate her steps; my toes touching the ground, my ankles high in the air, just like someone wearing heels. It was just my imagination, but I recall a saying that *where there is a dream, there is a miracle*. To this day, I always say, 'The higher the heels the higher the standards.'

Those shoes motivated me to love my schoolbooks because I wanted to wear them and be associated with greatness. One day, in grade six, I was sitting under our mahogany tree with my grandparents, explaining to my grandmother about my teacher's shoes. I told her, 'I would love to study and be like her. I want to live in a town, and use body lotions, just like my teacher.' Suddenly, my grandfather interrupted and shouted, 'ENOUGH … please tell this little girl that this is not America. She is allowed to study but she must not overdo it. And what's so special about those so-called shoes she's always talking about? Knock some sense into her head.' My grandfather's words *pissed me off*. I often ask myself why he talked that way about issues related to women's empowerment, but I haven't been able to find a satisfactory answer.

Isn't it strange how negative times are always the easiest to remember? There were a couple of incidents that happened at school – moments of humiliation – that I still remember vividly today.

I was playing with other students in the school playground, when I heard a loud noise: *k … rrrr … iiiiiip*. Hearing that sound, I didn't realise that my uniform was torn. I had been wearing the same green uniform since I was in grade four and it was now grade seven. As I continued playing, I heard laughing. 'Hahahaha – look, your uniform is torn … we can see your underwear. Quick, cover yourself before boys come …' Those were the voices of the girls I was playing with. My neighbour, Kundai, ran over with her jacket and wrapped it around my waist just as the school bell rang for us to go to assembly under our big, purple jacaranda tree. Everyone was happy as they were running to the assembly point.

I ran a little but then remembered my torn uniform. I started walking along the classroom walls, like a thief, so no one would notice that something was wrong with my uniform. As I was walking, somebody hit my back with a *thwwaaack*. A familiar voice said, 'What are you doing here, walking the walls like a lizard?' I turned around and showed Mrs Magondo my torn uniform. I saw pain in her eyes and realised she was holding back her tears. A couple of weeks later, she bought me a new uniform. The memory of this experience would continue to fuel my dreams, because whenever I wanted to sleep, the thought of poverty penetrated my brain like lightning, and I would wake up and study.

Time was ticking. I completed my grade seven exams and went to secondary school. It was in form two when I experienced my first period. I was sitting at my desk in my accounts class when I suddenly felt dampness between my legs, though I knew I wasn't urinating. I stood up and had the shock of my life; the bench and my uniform were soiled with blood. I didn't know what was happening to me. I screamed like a lunatic, my heart pounding in my chest like a djembe drum.

I'll never forget the words of my male teacher: 'Shut up! What a disgrace to the community and the lands. What kind of madness is this? You are unclean. You should not be around men. Take your bench and throw it outside. Clean up your mess and go home,' he shouted. I struggled, by myself, to take the heavy bench outside. I went home confused, trying to figure out what I did wrong. But alas, it was mother nature. I went back to school after a week but I was in the spotlight; everyone was making fun of me. I went home again because I couldn't take the humiliation. I returned the following day, but nothing changed. I did that for a week until I realised how difficult it would be for me to remain at that school.

I stayed home for about two months trying to figure out my wrongdoing. Of course, I couldn't find one. Worse, at home, my grandmother told me I should find old clothes or socks, anything that could absorb, since that was the only way for me to contain my period blood. To me at that moment, it was normal.

Another wise man once said *poverty will make you think that poverty is part of your culture – it only needs someone to remove the veil for you to see the other side of life.*

Nothing is as embarrassing as being made fun of by someone of your age. My aunt asked my grandmother whether it might be possible for me to change schools.

That's when I transferred to Matau High School, though I was still scared I would face the same fate. I ended up avoiding school whenever I had my period. I could miss five days of school every month due to the unavailability of feminine products.

When I started school there, people were always talking about Dr Trent and how wonderful she is, as well as her connection with Oprah Winfrey. I was fascinated and in awe of what I'd read about Oprah and wanted to discover more about Dr Trent. One day, I saw a lady was watching something on YouTube, and I peeped over her shoulder. She was watching a video entitled *Dear Daughter*. I heard the words, 'I know you have been wounded …' and felt as if she was talking to me on a personal level.

Those words were like small matches igniting an inferno inside me. I felt the urge to dust myself off and regain my confidence. I wanted to know who the woman was. I didn't have a cell phone, so I kept being curious, wanting to learn more about this woman.

I finished my O-level with flying colours and proceeded to A-level. I would always tell my history teacher that 'one day I will go to university', however, he didn't believe me because of my *poverty* status. In my last term at school, I finally met the woman I had been longing to know more about.

She never disappoints! She gave us a lecture named *Girl Power*. She asked us an important question which shaped the way I think and the way I view the community now. Her question was … 'What breaks your heart … and what are you going to do about it?' I began to reflect on my life and found the thing that most broke my heart was that I had suffered *period poverty* and shame. What was left was what I intended to do about it.

There is a saying that *if you sit on a question, the answer will find you*. It kept haunting me, especially *at that time of the month*. When my period comes, the memories still appear vividly in my mind. I went on to university but was constantly wanting to change the situation in my community, whereby girls miss school because of menstruation.

I had an idea but didn't have funds to support it. However, I'd heard *that where there is an idea, the best thing is to start.*

When I was about to finish my degree, after being given a scholarship by Tererai Trent International, I remembered my mentor's words: *It's not about you, it's about the community and what impact you are making in the community.*

In 2023, when I was about to finish my tertiary education, I read a statement saying: *Just do it … what are you tripping for?*

I pitched my idea on my social media platforms that I was launching a *period poverty project* for the girls in my village. My goal is to secure enough sanitary pads to ensure no girl will miss school because of a period.

In June, I started fundraising. It was slow, though some people were responding. Tererai Trent International held an exchange program with the students from Oklahoma State University. I shared my story with some girls, because I have mastered the art of storytelling and believe everyone should always share their story.

A girl called Bryanna Nickel followed me and said she would help. The following day, Parker Perry connected, also wanting to help. That's when I realised, *Okay, I can do this.* When women come together amazing things happen.

The girls helped me to fundraise, and we managed to secure reusable and disposable pads for the girls. I haven't stopped smiling. What melts my heart most is a message I received from one of the girls. Ruvarashe shared with me how period poverty affected her and how the initiative brought so much positivity to her, because she used to live with *the regret of being a woman*. I saw myself in her and that gives me fuel to do more.

We were able to teach thirty-three girls to hand-sew reusable pads, so as to make the initiative more sustainable. This also taught them the idea of giving back. I told them that, 'When you sew another pad, give it to someone from your class, so that we can change the world for others.' The girls seemed to like the idea.

I will not stop until every girl in school no longer has to experience period poverty. I know what it's like to fight against period poverty because I suffered it. I've started with my province, and I won't stop until I reach every corner of Africa. I will make a difference.

FLORENCE KAYUNGWA

PHILANTHROPIST

Fundraiser who is fighting period poverty and shame in Hurungwe region, Zimbabwe, so as to make sure that no girl (student) is limited by her period.

PROFESSIONAL SUMMARY
- Experienced news anchor and producer at Pachikomo FM (98.6) voluntary.
- Network marketer part-time at Green World Group of Companies.
- Production manager (film and TV) intern.
- Graduate trainee Nrtv news reader and reporter (current).
- Philanthropist.

QUOTE
'Until the female lion becomes the historian of her own story, the tail of the hunt will glorify the hunter at the expense of the lioness.'

RECLAIM YOUR SELF-EXPRESSION TO BE YOUR MOST RADIANT SELF

Gaëlle Berruel

Gorgeous,

You're a diamond in the rough. Don't let anyone convince or influence you that you're not because they don't know you.

I see you, trying to believe in yourself, torn between overthinking and doubt, not seeing you as I see you, and despite it all, I know you're able to do it: reclaim your self-expression.

You crave to regain this ability but you can't figure out your next steps. However, you know one single thing: you have something to share with the world. Your voice, your work – they matter.

Are you hearing your intuition with a little nudge of encouragement, but you're still paralysed by your fears? Feeling torn between your desires and responsibilities, not having the confidence to take this leap of faith?

Why? Because you've never done it before FOR YOU.

The challenge is, you don't want to 'rock the boat' and question yourself, *Who am I to do this?*

But let me tell you, Gorgeous, what if you are the perfect person to do this?

What if, like Marianne Williamson said, you ask yourself, *Who am I to be brilliant, gorgeous, talented, fabulous? Actually, who are you* not *to be?*

Today, I have a special present for you. Reclaiming my self-expression, I did it, and I can show you the way.

It's unconventional and far away from the traditional path but I am the fullest expression of who I am – bold, visible and confident, unapologetically, and I wouldn't change it in any way.

GAËLLE BERRUEL

BECOME THE LEADER OF YOUR MIND

One of your superpowers is your mind. You're ambitious, smart and assertive. You learned to create your path in a world designed for men, and you managed to create your bubble of comfort and happiness.

The problem is, your calling is knocking on your door, and you feel trapped because you feel that you're meant for more.

And you're used to doing that – weighing the pros and cons, being super-uber analytical and staying vigilant, not taking any risk.

And when you feel you did it wrong, you rehearse the same situation for days in your head. I lost count of the times I did it working in corporate, overanalysing the situation at hand.

I was swimming in the self-sabotage sea and I didn't have a clue about it. I was getting in my way – BIG TIME.

But I knew there was a way. I couldn't put my finger on it, but I never stopped to believe it.

When I dived into the self-education world, I discovered it and I never looked back.

Gorgeous, there's a way to have your mind onboard to stretch your comfort zone (and be free to speak up confidently).

Your mind is like a Ferrari — either you drive it or it's going to drive you. I learned to lead my mind, not to let it lead me.

How? By understanding the language of my mind. I jump straight into it – neurosciences and neuroplasticity. This fantastic ability for our brain to create new neural patterns, change our beliefs and create our realities. And between me and you, it was like discovering Ali Baba's cavern full of treasure and wonder.

These treasures helped me make my mind work for me, not against me.

We all use a language to be heard and understood; the same applies to your mind. When you understand its language, you can speak to it and be guaranteed that it will receive your messages or instructions.

You start to become the leader of your mind when you apply these three principles:

- Place yourself as a non-judgemental observer: Allow yourself to listen to both of your voices, to make the distinction between your inner critical voice and your intuition. My inner critic or ego is critical, judgemental and can be mean. On the other hand, my inner voice is subtle, whispering encouragement, offering different perspectives to see the world or providing creative ideas. The key is not to take a stand, but just to listen so you learn to detach yourself from your thoughts.
- Understand and appreciate your ego: Instead of blaming it for your struggles, thank it for its amazing job of protecting you. I used to do the same, but this is not the solution. Your ego's purpose is to protect you at any cost, from any emotional risk. What does it mean? Each time you're going to entertain the idea of doing something different, new or risky, your ego will use a few ammunitions under its sleeve: your fears, your resistance to change and mind patterns, like over-thinking, doubt, perfectionism and so many more. The key, once again, is to recognise it, so you raise your awareness and learn how your mind functions. Instead of running away, as I used to, I now pause and interpret this as a sign that this is exactly my next step. Because behind any fear or resistance, your potential awaits. Let's be honest, our ego did a brilliant job until now. Now, that you understand its purpose, you can reclaim your freedom of choice to make another decision. This is true empowerment.
- Say yes to curiosity: This is a skill to cultivate for life, the one that leads me to delve into the self-education world. I've always been the kind of girl challenging the status quo, and my curiosity led me to where I am.

Curiosity helps you to stretch the capacity of your mind, to see things differently, shift your perspective and consider different points of view.

It will help you to expand your mindset, from a narrow mindset to a growth mindset, which is a real eye-opener. You'll see and recognise the opportunities, the potential, the possibilities. The result? Your potential is no longer a dream; it's at your fingertips.

SECOND STEP – BECOME A QUEEN

We are in a world designed for men. However, being a woman is a privilege, not a curse. We are biologically designed in a unique way, calling for revolutionary self-care and self-love.

Why? Because we've been conditioned to prioritise people's needs over our own, to self-silence, and this is detrimental to our health, happiness and career fulfilment.

The result? A mental and emotional struggle we've internalised for generations. But the great news is, you're part of the generation to break these societal narratives and stereotypes, restoring your self-worth and self-love.

There's another language to discover and learn – the language of your body. We're all inherently connected to it since our birth, but we don't always listen to its clues and signs. Most of the time, we ignore them.

So, let me show you how to become a queen and make peace with your body, for more harmony, safety and poise.

- Your Bliss-ipline (wellness routine): When I had the breakthrough that my body was my best friend and the direct link between me and my visibility, I felt so loved, because it changed, in one instant, my relationship with my body. From seeing my body as functional and never as toned as I wanted it to be, I relearned to tune into my body to understand its language. I dedicated time to creating more bliss with my Bliss-ipline. What does it entail? Each day, we are bombarded with requests, emails, demands and responsibilities, creating stress in our bodies and minds. The game-changer is to look after your body, so it can release the stress from a cellular level and come back to a state of being where calm confidence is your new standard as a queen. The next step is to make time in your calendar and make your Bliss-ipline non-negotiable. By blocking time in your calendar to meditate, have a walk or a gratitude practice, journal or do a workout, you're declaring that your self-love and joy matter. As Viola Davis said: 'You are the love of your life'. Gorgeous, honour it and make it non-negotiable.

- Your sense of safety: In a world where performance and hustling seem like the only solution for success, it is, for us, a direct door to burnout and emotional exhaustion in the long-term. Our hormones demand nourishment and our bodies demand feminine energy with deep rest. Your intuition is 'your angel', helping you bring back this harmony within your body. The more you'll be receptive to your body's clues and signs, the more your body will reveal to you its needs to be safe. For instance, your parasympathetic nervous system. When you feel stressed, tired or irritated, this internal system is your ally to go back to a state of peace, groundedness and serenity in a few minutes with the emotional freedom technique, essential oils or deep breathing.

- Forgive: It's the most liberating act you can do for yourself. Let me tell you why. Forgiving someone for what they did to you is not the act of condoning people's behaviour, but freeing yourself from the emotional charge of their behaviour to regain your emotional agency. These people who hurt you can't feel your anger, your hurt, your disappointment, so the onus is on you to choose forgiveness and freedom over pain and resentment. Forgive yourself also for your mistakes and inactions. Why? Because you did your best with the tools you had in the moment. You are neither omniscient nor omnipotent; you're an imperfect human being, evolving to be the best version of yourself.

BECOME A ROCKSTAR

This is my favourite part of this journey. Why? Because I believe, that you have something unique, special, that no-one can define but you. When you're willing to get to know yourself and recognise your allure, charisma and magnetism, something inside you is unlocked – the ability to show your brilliance, own it and inspire others to do the same.

You make your joy sacred and inspire the world to reconnect to it with gusto. As Maya Angelou said, "They may forget about what you said, they may forget about what you did, but they would never forget the way you make them feel".

The last step is to become a rockstar – in a nutshell, ignite your ability to shine like the diamond you are, and you can achieve this with these three tools:

- Protect your energy: What does it mean? You didn't work on yourself to be affected by people less conscious than you, prone to negativity and drama. Gorgeous, protect all the hard work you put in to have a positive mindset, do the inner work and elevate your personal growth. So, be assertive and surround yourself with people uplifting your energy, supporting you and believing in you. Play the detective like Miss Enola Holmes and find out what is draining or amplifying your energy. Carve out time to do what makes you feel good. It could be reading a book, having a stroll in a park or booking an energy healing session. Regardless of what it is, make sure to protect your energy and keep your vibes high. Your energy is your currency.
- Cultivate your faith: Your faith is the energy that will keep you carrying on, no matter what you see, or the challenges and obstacles you face. When you commit to keeping your faith alive, you start to believe in what you don't see, creating a wave of possibility that opportunities will flow to you easily, joyfully and effortlessly. Whatever you want to call it – the Universe, higher power or God – the belief to be supported, loved and encouraged beyond measure will help you to persevere, bounce back, believe in yourself and know that you're never alone. You have a one-of-a-kind extraordinary cheerleader, and

as Gabby Bernstein says, he has your back. I wouldn't be where I am without my faith, without believing that the universe is guiding me to be the fullest expression of who I am every day.

Ignite your authenticity: It's one of the choices I made a few years ago that turned my life upside-down and opened incredible doors of opportunities for me. Being authentic means being true to your own personality, values and spirit, regardless of the pressure you're under to act otherwise. The word authentic originates from the Greek *authentikos*, which means genuine, and from *authentes*, one acting on one's own authority. When you're authentic, you act from your own authority, and as a result, you are seen as an authority.

GAËLLE BERRUEL

Gaëlle is an award-winning visibility coach, a motivational speaker and a wellness expert.

She is the CEO and founder of A Rockstar Mindset.

She's also a UK ambassador for Psychologies magazine, inspiring and motivating readers to create a life they love through the online Life Labs platform.

After ten years working in the banking industry, she created her visibility consultancy, A Rockstar Mindset, to help women leaders (specifically successful business owners and senior/executive women) become the rockstar of their life: bold, visible and confident unapologetically.

How? By helping women leaders become visible, so they are recognised for their work and value.

What separates Gaëlle from other coaches is her infectious positive energy, her rockstar mindset and her firm belief that every woman deserves to be the fullest expression of who they are (authentic, unapologetic and aligned) and financially free.

Because of this, clients feel supported, take inspired actions and achieve their professional dreams. Inspired by the world of neurosciences, positive psychology and wellness, Gaëlle created her holistic system, The Rockstar Woman Framework, which helps women be visible and recognised so they can shine unapologetically.

Gaëlle was featured in magazines like Psychologies, Medium, and Entrepreneurs Herald and gave talks at Vodafone, Monica Vinader and the Women Federation for World Peace.

PAGES OF HOPE
EMPOWERING CHILDREN TO CHANGE THE WORLD
Heather McCarthy

I was only five or six years old when our family took a road trip to the state's capital, where history whispered through the air and the sun painted golden hues on the cityscape. I remember walking along a vast area lined with tall shade trees. The scent of freshly cut grass wafted through the air and the distant hum of city life blended with the rustling leaves overhead. My parents unpacked our picnic basket beneath the welcoming shade of the mall's ancient oak trees. As we settled onto the soft grass, the simple pleasures of a homemade lunch unfolded – sandwiches, fresh fruit, and ice-cold waters were passed between me and my siblings. Laughter danced among the leaves as we chatted and played in the warmth of a perfect summer's day.

Other families picnicked nearby, children played and couples strolled hand in hand. Yet, among the vibrant tapestry of life, the less fortunate lingered on the fringes. It was my brother who asked my parents about a lone figure occupying a bench nearby. His tattered clothes and weary eyes spoke volumes about a life marked by hardship. My dad, his eyes always reflecting a genuine compassion, yet a stern voice commanding us to listen, explained how blessed our family was to have a meal to eat, comfortable clothing and a home for shelter. He suggested we look around to find someone to share our lunches with, adding that a small act of kindness can make a big difference.

I remember being both nervous and reluctant, but following the lead of my older brothers, I approached the man my brother had previously pointed out, extending a portion of my lunch. His eyes, initially fixed on the ground, met mine. In that silent exchange, a connection transcended our differences. I smiled, and the man, grateful and surprised, managed a nod that spoke volumes. That encounter, a small but profound moment, left an indelible mark on my young heart. It wasn't just about sharing a meal, it was the realisation my dad was right; even the smallest act of kindness could connect the divided.

The memory of that day lingered for years, a silent beacon guiding my path. It became the cornerstone of my aspiration to create a ripple effect of kindness in a world often turbulent with inequality. I believe this memory led me to a career in education, driven by the desire to foster empathy and compassion in young minds. Teaching seemed to be the canvas upon which I could paint the values instilled by that family vacation so long ago, a platform to nurture empathy, kindness and a sense of responsibility toward others.

Eventually, my journey in education led me to the corridors of the school library. Here, literature became not just a tool for learning but a bridge to service and understanding. I realised the power of stories to ignite empathy, to provoke thought and to inspire action. It is not just about books, it's about harnessing their narratives to cultivate a generation of changemakers.

Connecting literature to service learning became my calling, a synergy where reading and learning are not confined to the pages of a book, but expanded into real-world actions – actions that echo the simple gesture of sharing a sandwich. It was in this realm of service learning that I found my true passion; empowering students to recognise the power of their voices, regardless of their age, and fostering a belief that each small step, each word spoken for good, has the potential to transform lives.

A NEW LENS: MOTHERHOOD'S TRANSFORMATIVE VIEW

My journey of connecting literature to service learning started small, with local acts of kindness and service to others. My students and I held food, clothing and shoe drives. We made cards for children who were ill, and for the elderly who needed a friend. We read daily picture books to create videos and podcasts about diversity, equity and inclusion. We started small, knowing it is the smallest acts of kindness that can have the biggest impact.

After years of teaching my students to recognise the power of their voices and encouraging them to create positive change, I became a mother. My beliefs in community service and empathy took on an entirely new dimension. This desire to make the world a better place was exponentially compounded. Holding my child, staring into her face, everything changed. Viewing the world through this fresh lens of motherhood revealed a deeper layer of empowering others to recognise the power of their voice and actions. It was a shift that became even more profound five days into motherhood. After bringing my daughter home from the hospital, I was called by the doctors who informed me there was an irregularity in her newborn pre-screening. She had an appointment with the genetic team downtown the very next morning, where we received the diagnosis of Propionic Acidemia, a rare metabolic condition. Three and a half years later, our son was also born with the same diagnosis. I hesitate even to bring up their diagnosis because it does not define them. The journey of Propionic Acidemia is their story to tell.

However, from a mother's perspective, hearing that your children have a rare medical condition unearthed an unwavering determination to shape a world that embraces empathy and understanding, especially for those facing unique challenges. Through the lens of nurturing a child with specific needs, I discovered a new-found strength to advocate, educate and foster empathy on a broader scale for all causes. I'm driven by the belief that a more empathetic world is an imperative mission – one that motherhood gifted me and one I will tirelessly pursue.

A GLOBAL AWAKENING

While having children changed my perspective on so many levels, it was a single journey to Simbi, Rwanda, that was my global awakening. After my students and I read Linda Sue Park's novel *A Long Walk to Water*, we began studying the water crisis in Africa and learning how young girls walk each day to collect dirty, contaminated water for their families. This prompted me to travel to Africa to witness this plight.

Walking alongside a family in Simbi was a transformative moment, etched into the deepest recesses of my memory. As I traversed the dusty paths, witnessing the daily struggles of young girls burdened with the arduous task of fetching contaminated water, an overwhelming wave of emotions engulfed me. These resilient young souls, entrusted with a duty that should never be theirs, struck a chord which resonated to the core of my being. Their footsteps, tirelessly tracing the same path multiple times a day, were meant to sustain life but subsequently endangered the health of their families. The gravity of their plight reshaped my perspective in profound ways, challenging my understanding of adversity and resilience. It was a gut-wrenching realisation – the sheer disparity between their struggles and the privileges I took for granted.

During my time in Rwanda, I bore witness not only to the effects of water and the tragedies of the Rwandan genocide, but also to the unwavering faith in humanity that persisted amidst the ravages of history. In one of the most rural and impoverished communities, with hunger reflected in the children's eyes, I witnessed an act of pure kindness. A child selflessly divided the last piece of candy among others, ensuring each child savoured a taste, embodying the spirit of sharing and compassion that transcended their hardships. Their clothing, ripped and stained, clearly portrayed the stories of struggle, but their smiles spoke volumes – echoes of gratitude, love and an unshakeable spirit. It was the installation of a pipeline, distributing fresh mountain drinking water to thousands across multiple villages that showed me the transformative power of hope and resilience.

In the wake of these experiences, my perception of adversity underwent a seismic shift. The haunting statistic that one in five children in

Africa succumb to the horrors of unclean water and perish before the age of five echoed in my mind. Reflecting on my own two children back home, safe and sheltered in an environment blessed with clean drinking water, ample food, access to health care and educational resources, the contrast became painfully apparent. Being a mother had always been a profound part of my identity, but this trip to Rwanda heightened my awareness of the privileges my children and I enjoy. It was an emotional awakening – a realisation that my motherhood extended beyond my own family; it connected me to a global community of mothers striving for a safer, healthier world for their children.

Returning home, reflecting on the adversities and the unwavering resilience, compassion and hope that I witnessed, I carried with me not just memories, but a resounding sense of responsibility. The experiences of witnessing struggles halfway across the globe fuelled my passion to ignite change and amplify my efforts in empowering children to realise their innate potential as agents of change.

HEARTFELT INITIATIVES: STUDENTS LEADING WITH EMPATHY

The Rwandan experience bridged continents, linking our local service projects with global realities. Witnessing children risking their health for a basic necessity, I realised the urgency to amplify our efforts beyond boundaries.

The heart of our initiatives lay not just in the acts themselves but in the cultivation of empathy, fuelled by the unique voices and choices of my students. Their passions became the driving force behind every endeavour, transforming each project into a journey of empathy and understanding. With the leadership of the students, we now host 6km races, the average distance the girls in Africa have to walk for water, raising thousands of dollars with each race. The students hold an annual meal packaging event, helping package hundreds of thousands of meals to be delivered to local food pantries, schools, veteran organisations and places in need. A group of girls initiated a sewing club to send clothing to local, national and global organisations. When a student had a sibling going through treatment at the local children's hospital, we rallied together to create another service learning project. They used our library's technology resources to make interactive picture books for the children at the hospital. The students have created prosthetics for vulnerable children and have upcycled airline seats into fashion projects.

Every meal packaged, every step taken in those 6km races, every stitch sewn into a dress and every interactive book created, is not about the physical actions, it is about fostering a realisation that their actions hold the power to bridge divides, connecting their hearts to the needs of others. The power of empathy lay at the core of their actions, propelling them to envision a world reshaped by kindness and compassion.

There is a spark ignited within them as they realise the profound impact of their actions. In these experiences, their voices ring loud and clear, shaping the projects from inception to fruition. Their choices are not dictated but revered, allowing them to infuse their unique perspectives into each initiative. This ownership magnifies the impact, instilling in them a profound sense of agency and responsibility.

Each year the students come with more ideas, projects, and service learning initiatives, all of which resonate as powerful lessons in empathy. Understanding realities starkly different from our own became catalysts for reflection, urging students to step into others' shoes and amplify their commitment to uplift those in need. Whether addressing local issues or extending their reach globally, these initiatives serve as powerful conduits for students to exercise their empathy, voice and choice in crafting a world fuelled by compassion and understanding.

NARRATIVES OF CHANGE: EMPOWERMENT THROUGH LITERATURE

Throughout this journey, the power of literature to transform empathy into action emerges as a central theme. Literature is not merely a collection of stories; it is a gateway to understanding, compassion and service. I have witnessed the synergy between literature and service learning, realising that without diverse narratives, the seeds of empathy might never find fertile ground to flourish.

As I navigate the complexities of education, championing service learning projects born from the pages of beloved stories, I shudder at the growing challenge of book censorship and banning. The surge in attempts to silence voices, particularly those representing the BIPOC and LGBTQ communities, threatened the very essence of inclusive education.

The stark reality is, without access to diverse and inclusive books, the tapestry of empathy woven through service learning projects will unravel. The stories we read serve as catalysts, inspiring students to grasp the complexities of the world and to empathise with diverse perspectives. My advocacy for defending the freedom to read is not just a battle for intellectual liberty; it is a fight for the heartbeat of empathy within our educational landscape. Access to inclusive literature is the cornerstone, the vital link, between the stories that ignited empathy within my students and the service projects that translated their empathy into tangible action.

I will ardently fight for equity, diversity and inclusion, recognising that every child deserves access to books that mirror their identities, while offering windows into the lives and experiences of others. The pursuit of intellectual freedom intertwines seamlessly with the quest for empathetic understanding. In the walls of the library, literature ceases to be solely about stories – it becomes a catalyst for service and understanding.

ECHOES OF EMPATHY: A CALL TO YOUNG VOICES

In the patchwork of memories, one pivotal moment stands timeless – a small gesture of sharing a sandwich with a stranger. It was a whisper in time, echoing the timeless truth, that every act of kindness, no matter how seemingly insignificant, carries the power to kindle hope, bridge divides and ignite change.

To every child, I extend this unwavering truth – a truth that resonated in my heart since that unforgettable vacation – you matter, your actions count and you have the power to change the world. Within the intricate web of experiences chronicled here, I have witnessed the power of empathy, the transformative force that unites hearts and shapes destinies.

Empathy is the cornerstone of understanding, the compass guiding us through the labyrinth of differences and the catalyst for a more compassionate world. In the myriad of challenges that confront us, from censorship to the battle for equity and inclusivity, empathy stands as our beacon, our North Star, illuminating the path forward.

Together, let's champion service, let's fight for access to literature that mirrors our identities and unlocks the doors to unfamiliar worlds. Let's nurture the seeds of empathy within our hearts and minds, cultivating a garden where compassion blooms abundantly.

For in this journey, from the childhood memory that sparked a flame within me, to motherhood, to the adventures that traversed continents and transformed perspectives, I have witnessed one resounding truth – empathy, cultivated through the pages of stories and amplified through service, is our currency for change.

Heather McCarthy is an educational leader who uses her passion for literature to spread the message of love, empathy and equality through service learning projects with her students. For over twenty years, Heather has been inspiring young children to create a brighter future for their community, nation and world. Heather McCarthy has been named the Most Inspirational Educator for Illinois, has won the Distinguished Alumni Award from her high school and the Distinguished Service to Society Award from her university. Heather has won numerous awards including the Community Supporter of the Year Award, the Distinguished Women of Excellence Award and the Dr Tererai Trent Award for her humanitarian work. She won the Mover and Shaker Award from the American Library Association as one of the top up-and-coming individuals from around the world who is innovative, creative and making a difference in librarianship. Heather has also been nominated for the global award entitled Women Changing the World under the category of education.

Heather leads by example volunteering locally, nationally and on a global scale. She has travelled to South Africa and Kenya while working on clean water projects in Rwanda and Malawi. She volunteered at an elephant sanctuary in Chiang Mai, Thailand, assisting at the elephant hospital and taking on the role of a mahout. Heather volunteers her time at the local children's hospital and for an organisation bringing books to youth in prison to encourage imagination, self-determination and connection to the outside world. All of her volunteer work is brought back to her students motivating them to use their voices for good, serve others

HEATHER MCCARTHY

and ultimately make the world a better place. Heather's educational leadership and unwavering commitment to giving back to others have helped her students become leaders, activists and changemakers.

WHEN YOUR NAME BECOMES YOUR CALLING

Iris Mhlanga

"Help ... please ... somebody ... anybody ... this man needs help!"

I was on my knees in the alley outside the grocery store, trying to help a man, who appeared unconscious. His wheelchair had fallen backward, and he was lying with his back on the ground, still in the chair. As he was starting to come around, I somehow got his wheelchair upright and gave him a sip of Coca-Cola, which made a difference. He was able to explain that he was homeless and hadn't eaten for two days. I fed him some bread, and continued to comfort him while I called my good friend, Kenny, an ambulance technician, asking his advice on how I could support this man.

Soon, there was quite a crowd of people watching, but no-one was helping, ... and I was astounded. A lady called out to me, "he doesn't like help, you'll regret this!" But I couldn't leave him. "You've saved my life," he said.

It was September 2018, and part of the reason I couldn't walk away, is that 'helping others' is pretty much in my DNA. I was born into a family of helpers who had a passion for supporting the less privileged; many of my family members worked to support vulnerable people and communities. My father, a local businessman, had been given the honorary title of "City Father" for the work he did in his community and as president of the local Highlanders Football Club. After he died, I discovered he'd been paying school fees for hundreds of children.

I was raised by my mother's side of the family, with 8 siblings, and we were always taught to care for others. We looked out for one another, and I too, was supported by the family when my son was born with bilateral talipes (double clubfoot). It was tough at times raising a disabled son, but through the kindness of strangers, he was able to have an operation to improve his condition. We travelled to Zambia and I learnt a lot about patience, love and giving through the experience, seeing children struggling with far worse disabilities than my son.

My grandmother had Parkinson's Disease in her later years, and because of the way I cared for her and others, she joked that I was like a *mother to all*. I was ok with that. After all, my name is Nozizwe, and literally translated means "mother of nations". It's interesting in our family how our names have helped mould the people we are and the work we do. As an example, my brother Lizwi is a PR consultant. Lizwi literally translates to "voice".

Another reason I couldn't walk away, may surprise some readers! Just the week before this incident, I had been going through a bit of a hard time. My father had passed away in 2016 and I had been called to a meeting with the family lawyers about inheritance issues. On the way back, I called into a church and chatted with the Pastor, Francis Kwabena Asiedu. He told me I "would one day meet a homeless disabled man and that experience would be the birth of something mind-blowing."

I discovered that Mr Ncube wheeled himself in a broken wheelchair, 20km from Bulawayo Homeless Shelter to spend the day in Bradfield, and then wheel himself all the way back again - every day! Why? He said he, "liked being around nice people." I was surprised. Those people had stood by and not helped him. I promised I would take care of him. When I arrived the next day, he was eating scraps out of an old rusty bin, so I began by cooking meals for him … and soon … his friend, and another friend …. and their friend's friends were being fed too. Over time, it became hundreds!

After the first incident, I put a post out on Facebook, a bit of rant if I'm honest, about what had happened and how people had walked past. That post went viral! It turned out the Bradfield community did want to help after all and suddenly there was plenty of support to help the homeless. It all happened quite quickly but I discovered I could support Mr Ncube with more than just food. Someone called me offering a wheelchair but told me they didn't want any publicity. Two days later, not just one wheelchair, but a truck full of food, clothes and wheelchairs arrived. I was shocked.... What was I going to do with all of that? I called him back and said I wasn't sure what to do with everything he'd sent. "Just wait and see," he said, "you can't just help one person." This person became an inspiration in my life and his donations changed the trajectory of what I was doing to support people in those early days.

When I first gave the new wheelchair to Mr Ncube, he tried to refuse. "You're doing too much," he said. But actually, he was loving the attention. "I thought I'd been forgotten," he added. He started calling me *Mummy*, and I was ok with that. I am Nozizwe after all.

By the end of 2018, just about 3 months later, I was supporting so many people and it was spreading like wildfire. But something came along to knock the wind from my sails. My beautiful daughter, Ana, was rushed to hospital in a diabetic coma and was on life support for several days, and my son, Christian, needed me too. I had to be a mother to my children and care for my family first. I felt I couldn't take care of anyone else. I put up a post again on Facebook and reached out to the Bradfield community. This time the response was amazing, and the community stepped up to support the hundreds we were now feeding.

When my daughter stabalised and we returned home, I discovered I'd been nominated for a Charity Hero award. My father's lawyers heard about was happening, and were impressed, yet concerned at the speed with which things were moving. They wanted to support me by setting up a registered not-for-profit organisation. "You're going to be a mother to all," they said. And I was ok with that. The trust was born using proceeds from my inheritance, from both my father's and mother's families, and a few dollars from well-wishers.

IRIS MHLANGA

I met Mr Ncube in September 2018 and on 21st May 2019, my application to set up the trust was approved. Another funny thing; the application for the trust was put to the courts just a few days before, and the lawyers told me to expect it to take several months for approval. However, my pastor, again, predicted it would happen in three days – and it did! The lawyers were astounded!

WHEN YOU'RE ON THE RIGHT PATH – THINGS HAPPEN QUICKLY!

Now, in 2024, my day to day involves sourcing donations for the soup kitchens, elderly people and orphans under our care. I seem to be good at getting the donations we need and I'm grateful and thankful for all the organisations and companies who regularly and generously donate food items and other necessities, be it clothing, stationery, wheelchairs and other mobility aides. If a charity is looking for 1000 loaves of bread, I'm the person they call. We also partner with other organisations to set up medical outreach programmes providing free health care to vulnerable communities.

Basically, Nozizwe Trust is a community effort. We jump in where we feel we can assist, countrywide, with the help of people from Bradfield and the greater Bulawayo community where I live.

Currently, we have more than 5000 people supported under Nozizwe **Trust:**

- We partner with a few other larger organisations, by sourcing food items for Mustard Seed Communities Zimbabwe and King George School for the Disabled.
- The Mustard Seed Communities soup kitchens feed 1200 children per day at 5 different locations.
- We have over 100 elderly widows under our care who we assist with their day to day needs if they are unable to work due to their age. The eldest is 114 years old.

- We pay school fees for 1000 orphans at various schools around the country; the first school we supported was Kent Primary School in Mhondoro Zimbabwe.
- We adopted a ward at a mental health institution (Ingutsheni Hospital) in Bulawayo, where there are 20 special needs patients with severe mental and physical disabilities.
- We are involved in food outreach programmes with an organisation called Feed the City Zimbabwe
- We're setting up community gardens in the Sigola area and drilling boreholes to alleviate water issues in various communities across the country.
- We set up water tanks at the local rubbish dump (Ngozi mine) where we feed 340 vulnerable children who live in the dumpsite.
- From time to time, funds allowing, we donate to random appeals and requests we get from around the country.

It always surprises me, when I look back, how quickly things can move forward when you're on the right path. A lot of what the Trust has achieved has been down to the people I have been blessed to meet on this journey. If I hadn't been contacted by Aboobaker Omar, when Mr Ncube first needed a wheelchair, we may not be supporting the numbers we are today. I was blessed to call Baker (as we called him) my friend; he even became a father figure and best friend to my daughter, as he too had diabetes. We were devastated when he passed from kidney failure in 2021 and I promised I would continue his journey. He passed out one morning whilst loading his truck full of donations to deliver to a community 500kms away. He was a philanthropist in the true sense of the word, giving so much to the greater community with humility, never wanting any recognition for his efforts. He and his driver, Joe Moosa, taught me that you can never help, "just one person," when you are prepared to care.

There have been so many wonderful people who make a difference every day in the lives of the people we support. It takes a dedicated team to coordinate and support the number of people we do, and I hope I show my gratitude and say thanks to them every day. I am amazed at the international exposure we are now receiving for the work we do, often in the 'back of beyond'! It's inspiring to receive letters and messages of encouragement from all over the world.

I never really think about who is watching; for me, the biggest achievement is seeing a big smile on someone's face. People become like family when we're out there and I enjoy meeting people from all walks of life irrespective of the challenges they face. I'm just happy to be the reason someone smiles. I feel like I am *mother to many*, and I'm ok with that!

IRIS MHLANGA

Iris Nozizwe Mhlanga is an extraordinary woman who has dedicated her life to making a positive impact in the lives of others. She is the founder and philanthropist behind the Nozizwe Mother of Nations Trust, an organisation that aims to uplift and empower women and children in Zimbabwe and beyond.

Born Iris Zemza Nozizwe Mhlanga, she grew up in Bulawayo Zimbabwe. From a young age, Nozizwe had a deep sense of compassion and a burning desire to help those in need. She witnessed firsthand the struggles and hardships faced by women and disabled children in her community, and this inspired her to take action.

Nozizwe founded the Mother of Nations Trust in 2018 with the goal of providing education, health care and economic opportunities to marginalised women, men and children. Through her organisation, she has implemented various programs and community initiatives that have made a significant difference in the lives of countless individuals.

One of the key areas of focus for the Mother of Nations Trust is education. Nozizwe firmly believes that education is the key to breaking the cycle of poverty and empowering individuals to create a better future for themselves and their communities. The organisation provides scholarships and educational resources to underprivileged children, enabling them to access quality education and pursue their dreams.

Health care is another crucial aspect of the Mother of Nations Trust's work. Nozizwe understands that access to health care is a fundamental right that should be available to all. Her organisation has partnered with like-minded organisations and established medical clinics, doctors and mobile health care units in remote areas, ensuring that even the most vulnerable individuals have access to basic health care services.

In addition to education and health care, the Mother of Nations Trust also focuses on economic empowerment. Nozizwe believes that by providing women with the tools and resources to become financially independent, they can break free from the cycle of poverty and contribute to the development of their communities. The organisation offers vocational training programs as well in various parts of Zimbabwe.

IT IS NEVER TOO LATE

Janette Salmi

'I don't think you know what you have let yourself in for!' A look of *I'm sorry and thank you* rolled into one, looking right at me as I replied, 'Yes, I do – and it is a privilege and an honour.' Well, I thought I knew. It WAS a privilege and an honour, but the events over the ensuing five years were all joyous, bumpy, distressing and enlightening, and I would not trade them for the world.

Let me take you back. Geoff 'Tangle-tongue' Mack, the Australian singer/songwriter who wrote the iconic song 'I've Been Everywhere' was my precious Uncle Geoff – a man I loved dearly and admired and respected on many different levels.

His wife, Tabby Francis, was a remarkable eccentric with a wicked sense of humour, energetic on the dance floor, and a generous and always grateful soul. They both came to live with my husband and me in 2014. Uncle Geoff was already in his nineties, and Auntie Meg (as we lovingly called her) was still in her late eighties.

Sadly, Uncle Geoff passed away in July of 2017 at the ripe old age of ninety-four, and Auntie Meg went to join him in February 2020 on my birthday. She was ninety-three. A bit cheeky, I thought, but knowing her the way I did, I could hear her saying, 'Happy birthday – I release you from this responsibility.' It was quite beautiful when I allowed that to sink into my heart.

During their years with us, we were enriched by their stories, wisdom and advice. The joy of sharing their insights after a lifetime of rich experiences, along with many challenges and solutions, will remain with my family and me forever. What a true blessing and legacy they have left us.

My Aunty Meg and Uncle Geoff were still on stage entertaining at eighty years of age. What great role models they were. IT IS NEVER TOO LATE.

Humans are very complex beings. Each one of us has many facets.

I came into the world as a baby. I hear you saying, *How unusual!* Let me reassure you that I grew into a little girl, morphed into a complex teenager and blossomed into adulthood. The first twenty-one years saw many changes, emotions, decisions and perceptions of who I was and who I became. My first roles were as a daughter, granddaughter, niece, sister and cousin. Each of those roles is presented in a variety of different ways. I'm already quite complex.

Working in the international hotel world in public relations opened up many new opportunities and opportunities for growth. Some special lifetime friends were birthed, and the massive shift into adulthood began.

The following season saw me become a wife; I travelled extensively for three years, coming home with many lessons, experiences and perceptions at a whole new level. Marrying someone from a different culture certainly opened my eyes to new ways of viewing situations. I learned that what is correct, polite and acceptable in one country could prove very different in another. The complexities continue to grow.

Back on Australian soil, it was time to settle.

In the next chapter, I became a mother, an aunt, a sister-in-law and a godmother. They were very nurturing years and some of my favourites. I loved my four children more than life itself, and I was so proud of them – each unique in their own way. Life is not without struggles, but some of the best lessons are learned through effort. I learned early on that if you want to be strong, you need difficulties to become strong; if you seek wisdom, you need problems to learn from or solve.

If you aspire for courage, then be prepared for dangers to overcome, and if you want love aside from a loving family and friends, you need people to help. I quickly learned to look for the lessons, embrace them and not feel sorry for myself when life dished out challenges I did not like.

Once all my children were in school, I was encouraged to turn a corner and embrace a new and exciting adventure. I was in my forties, but IT was NEVER TOO LATE, so I embraced it wholeheartedly as I entered the world of education. With a bachelor of education, I began a career in teaching, which saw me teach in primary school, middle school, and later, secondary school. I continued to study and learn through many professional development workshops, seminars, conferences and master's of education. This led me to work in several coordination roles before becoming a deputy and retiring as a dean of students, which was my favourite role. IT IS NEVER TOO LATE.

This chapter also saw each of my children step up to become independent in their own world. There were three weddings and nine grandchildren that blessed our wonderful family. How fast this all unfolded.

As previously shared, it was during this time that my beautiful aunt and uncle stepped into the final chapter of their lives. I was in the very honourable position of supporting them throughout their last years. They remained in their family home for over sixty years. We were able to engage a provider in their hometown of Sydney, NSW, Australia, where we met some fantastic people. I want to mention Victoria, my main communication channel, as she provided very committed and thorough support.

Working as a dean of students, my life was busy and complete, and having a support person engaged on the level Victoria did, was terrific and very appreciated. However, we did reach a point where some serious decisions needed to be made.

Having had a lengthy hospital experience and a month in respite, we decided to bring them to Queensland to live with us. We had given them both some time together in an aged care facility for a month and although a very beautiful place with excellent staff, it was not the right way for them to live the final years of their lives.

December 2014 saw them move, and so began another chapter in all our lives. It was a significant and life-changing season for us all.

In December 2016, I retired from education. Thank goodness I did, as in 2017, my husband was diagnosed with lung cancer, and in July 2017, my precious Uncle Geoff passed away. My poor aunt's dementia escalated, and difficult times presented themselves. In 2020, my aunt had deteriorated to a point where we could not manage her pain as effectively or comfortably as would have been ideal, so on the recommendation of our doctor, we placed her into a hospice where she experienced the most dignified end to her life. I will be forever grateful to the staff who looked after her, and me, until she finally joined her precious husband in February 2020.

My years of caring for Aunty Meg and Uncle Geoff, and my experiences, made me passionate about the aged care and disability space. I could only do a little as I was retired and too old, OR WAS I?

To imagine that I would be engaging in the building of a business in my retirement years – in an industry I had experienced but had no training in – was not on my radar in any way at all. Yet here I was. IT IS NEVER TOO LATE.

To say I was being encouraged and gently pushed is an understatement. I was so naive and extremely idealistic but very passionate, and as life has it, the lessons came like an erupting volcano. Some are enlightening and encouraging, others disappointing and, dare I even say, at times, soul-destroying, but the gaining of wisdom, strength and integrity are often couched in these challenging experiences.

That is life, though. Isn't it? We all have seasons of growth, which come in all different shapes and forms.

To find your purpose in life is a gift. I wish we could all accomplish this; to travel in the lane we were destined to travel in, to impact the world exactly how we were designed to and to become the best version of ourselves no matter what.

WOMEN MAKING A DIFFERENCE

Mother Teresa is a great role model for us all. She became aware of the enormous suffering that surrounded her, and as she engaged and worked closely, she eventually realised that her purpose in life was to work and serve 'the poorest of the poor'. She became a role model of charity, compassion and selflessness, making an enormous impact. To the homeless and destitute, she is the beacon that gives hope to their desperate existence. She made a massive impact on many people's lives. She changed the world and inspired so many in her way. She was criticised and humiliated, but that didn't deter her. Mother Teresa devoted her life to caring for the sick, poor and disadvantaged. In the process, she challenged stereotypes, broke boundaries and taught us the true essence of charity.

Working with like-minded people is invigorating and stimulating. I have learned so much and continue to grow and evolve. Some ask why I would be doing such a mammoth task in my seventies, but why not? IT IS NEVER TOO LATE.

It is taking all my life experiences and the opportunity to pass on the prudence and wisdom of the years, instilling it into a business of relationships and ripple a positive impact throughout many lives. Influence is an honour, and sharing it with those close to me, for them to share it with all those they engage with, can have a massive force on our society, leaving a legacy for future generations.

The wisdom of the ages is something many do not recognise as readily as once upon a time. Still, the discipline of wise behaviour, wise thoughtfulness and integrity can be modelled and taught to future generations. Discretion, understanding and discernment guard and guide us. A healthy sense of wisdom regarding the moment's needs enables us to be great listeners, sensitive to the moment, available for relationships to flourish and to have a keen sense of the root causes of challenges.

To watch others learn, humble themselves, grow and give back is an honour. We believe that mistakes are lessons. Learn from them. Do what needs to be done with them to succeed, pivot and change.

Someone recently asked me if this was the most joyful time of my life. It didn't take much thought to respond – *it is*. I have come to a season where I can be the real me. Finally, I can be me; I can facilitate change, and I can leave my legacy. This excites me and inspires me every single day.

He added, 'Surely your legacy is to enjoy retirement?' Absolutely not! The timing is perfect for what I am doing now.

I must master it one step at a time. It is always possible to start afresh. Dare I reiterate that it is NEVER TOO LATE to use the life experience incurred during the preceding decades and the strength of character developed through the many challenges, experiences and opportunities both missed and engaged in. I sincerely hope others will watch and follow in my footsteps.

Key lessons I have learned include establishing boundaries – I now have them. It took a long time and many years of people-pleasing, but my personal and professional boundaries are now clear and operational. Once I realised that there would always be critics, no matter what choice I made, what direction I took or what decision I acted upon, I now only want those in my life who are supportive, respectful, and positive.

I've learned that in life, there is a purpose for everyone you meet. Some will challenge you, some use and abuse you, some will love you, and others will teach you. However, those who bring out the best in us are the ones who are truly important. They are the rare and remarkable people who prompt you why it is worth it.

With age comes credibility. What impact can you have on the world? What is your purpose? Save a lifetime of challenges, experiences and lessons. You have lived through decades of change. You have stories to impart, skill sets to embrace and teach and, dare I say, the wisdom of time and the ages. You cannot buy it or fast-track it; you have done your due diligence and embraced the life you were dealt with. This is the time of legacy. You must pass on the best of you, your abilities and your smarts.

You do not need to be famous or wealthy in money, but your richness alone is enough to make a massive difference. I challenge you to pick up your rod, make your mark on the world and show others how they can change the world in the most meaningful ways possible. If we all did our bit, the world would be far better. As women, we now have opportunities at our fingertips. My grandmother would have given anything to work, but my grandfather commented, 'No wife of mine will ever work.' That was how the culture was in those days. It was a slur on a man's manhood to have his wife take care of any income.

As I stated earlier, we are all COMPLEX. Use it to your advantage and make a massive IMPACT on this world. You are never too old; IT IS NEVER TOO LATE, and reinventions of self are magic. Go for it!

JANETTE SALMI

My name is Janette Salmi, and I live on the beautiful Gold Coast of Australia. I have been married to a Finn for almost fifty years and have four exceptional children (two girls and two boys) and nine beautiful grandchildren (three girls and six boys) – number ten on the way.

I have been blessed with some fantastic experiences, including challenges to overcome, but each led to where I am today. The unfolding of life is terrific, from a young woman working in public relations in an international hotel to three years travelling and working internationally, university study, earning a Bachelor of Education and a master's degree leading to a career in education teaching but culminating in executive positions including coordination roles, deputy and dean of students before retiring to care for my elderly aunt and uncle, and husband, who was suffering from lung cancer.

During this season of caring, I became passionate about the aged care and disability industry, which led to the birth of 'The Dignified Movement – A Lighthouse for Change', ensuring the development of life skills to enable our participants to grow and stay connected to their community feeling a sense of belonging. Similarly, in aged care, we assist a better life with the help of our lifestyle assistants with in-home care and community access.

Who starts a business in an industry unfamiliar to them in their retirement years? Hence the title of my chapter. It is never too late. I am well into this season, but my big dream is to build two hospices for adults and children. I would love this to be a charity so those in the final chapter of their life have support without worrying about money while having a painless and dignified end surrounded by those they love. Everyone deserves this. As part of the Lighthouse for Change, we intend to build a robust education platform attracting other like-minded individuals so that together, we can lift the standard of these industries.

I love what I do and hope to leave a lasting and memorable legacy for future generations.

SUCCESS OR FAILURE?

HOW A 5-FIGURE BUSINESS TAX DEBT CHANGED MY LIFE AND BUSINESS FOR GOOD

Justine McLean

What does success mean to you in this season of life and business? Now, it's the question I ask myself and my clients as we plan the next stage of business, but back when I started my first business, success was a concept I rarely considered. Sure, on some level, I wanted to achieve *success*, but deciding what that meant was never top of mind.

For me, success usually meant looking left and right, trying to measure up to everyone else.

Starting that first business in 1994 was about allowing me to stay home and care for our newborn son. It was trading time for money, and success back then usually meant a shower before midday! If I'm honest, the idea that I was running a business didn't enter the equation; I did the work, got paid and went about my day.

And that business idea worked … until it didn't. In 2002, now with four boys under seven, my husband David and I decided to partner up and open destination retail toy stores, plus an e-commerce business. We had story time, art classes and birthday parties, and sold beautiful, well-made toys. Simply trading time for money was no longer an option. Suddenly, we found ourselves with a whole lot of work to do to keep the business going, from ordering stock to managing staff, merchandising, marketing, tech stuff, operations and finances. We were overwhelmed and out of our depth. Success meant making it through the day with enough energy to do story time at night with our kids.

Our business took off quickly. We were busy making money, and the laundry list of things to do kept growing. And as any good partnership does, we divided up the jobs. Unfortunately, I got stuck with the finances; the job no-one else wanted to do.

As a creative person, the idea of doing numbers made me feel ill; I didn't do numbers! I almost failed maths at school, and apart from paying the household bills, taking on the business finances was not appealing at all. But someone had to do the work, and because we were bootstrapping this business, I had no choice but to step up and get the job done. I spoke to our accountant, who assured me it was as simple as registering the business for taxes and keeping track of the numbers. How hard could it be, right?

It's more complicated than you think!

Despite doing what I believed were all the right things, only a few years into the business, I got an email from my accountant which changed my life forever. I'll never forget it! I stared at that email in disbelief, sure that there must have been a big mistake. As I read and reread the email, panic started to rise. The number forty-two thousand, forty-two thousand, FORTY-TWO THOUSAND seemed to get larger each time I read it! After a frantic call to my accountant, my worst fear was realised: we owed $42,000 to the Australian Tax Office. There was no real explanation. We had no savings, and I had no idea how we would pay off the debt. Now I had to call David and tell him the news.

I sat in shame. What had I done wrong? Even though 'I didn't do numbers', I embraced the job I was given and was careful with every entry and expense. How had this happened? How did I get it SO wrong? At that moment, I felt stupid. My confidence was shattered, and the money story I'd been telling myself all my life was coming true. I couldn't be trusted with money and didn't deserve to have it. Who did I think I was starting such a big business? Our friends told us at the start that most businesses failed and they were right – we had failed!

You've heard the saying, you don't know what you don't know, and in this case, it was true. But it took a new accountant, many years and a lot of heartache before I finally forgave myself for my business money misstep. The debt was an accounting error not of my making, but in the aftermath of that massive tax bill and the struggle to pay it off, I realised there was a flaw in the system.

You see, in most countries around the world, we aren't taught how to manage our money, particularly when it comes to business, and more often than not, we run our businesses hoping for the best, sacrificing our time, energy and money in an attempt to achieve our definition of success.

At that moment, back in 2004, success was about paying off debt. Still, more than that, it became a journey to understand why I ended up in debt in the first place, so I would never let it happen again. My mum had taught me to fight in that positive, optimistic way only mums can, and that ingrained tenacity gave me the courage to go forward. So, instead of giving up and accepting that the $42,000 tax debt was a failure, I chose to reframe, go to the other extreme and view it as an opportunity.

I decided to learn everything I could about business finance.

I wanted to become a finance expert, and not in a boring, unrelatable way like so many finance professionals at the time, but in a practical, proactive and positive way, where I could serve my business and help other business owners too. I got educated, did one thousand hours of business activity statement (BAS) preparation working in an insolvency firm, and became a registered BAS agent. And that's where my business story truly begins.

In 2016, I opened a new business – helping small business owners with their bookkeeping and compliance and educating them on business money. My mission was simple; to help increase financial literacy so that business owners could pay themselves a wage and superannuation, as well as supercharge their profits, all while working in a business that fit their lifestyle.

For the first time in my business and life, I sincerely asked myself what success meant to me *now*, in this season. And when I knew the answer, I created a series of goals to help me achieve my definition of success. I kept the blinkers on because I knew the key to striving for success that was uniquely mine meant no more looking left and right, no more comparison. And as a trained money expert, one of my success measures had to be a financial goal, so that was in the mix too. I'd ask the same of my clients, and while their answers were often similar (they wanted to stop working for nothing, spend time with their kids or build a legacy and have an impact), each one of them had a unique reason for doing business.

Those success goals were vital because they gave my clients something to aim for and gave me insights into many businesses. Before long, I saw a pattern emerge. These incredibly talented people were good at what they did. They'd started in business to deliver beautiful products and services. However, only some of those business owners knew how to run a profitable business. When I looked behind the curtain, there was no cash flow, the pricing barely covered the cost of doing business, they had no savings, weren't paying themselves a wage and were one tax bill away from it all crashing down.

Something had to change.

I knew the key to their success was understanding the numbers and building solid financial foundations in their business. I also understood that building that financial foundation was more straightforward than it seemed. The barrier to entry was simply that these business owners needed to gain financial knowledge … so I set out to help.

The more businesses I worked with, the more significant the impact I witnessed. I helped talented women increase their financial knowledge, build the kind of businesses they'd only dreamt of and begin to change their lives, all with a tiny amount of financial expertise and a few minor tweaks.

GRACE'S STORY

One of my clients, Grace, a sought-after interior designer, is a beautiful example. At the time we started working together, Grace had been an industry professional for over twenty years. Grace was so in demand, she couldn't keep up with the workload, but at the end of each week, as she looked at her business bank account, there was little to show for her efforts. On the surface, she seemed to be making money, but in reality, her profit was less than 1%, and that was before she took a wage!

So, when we first started working together, I asked Grace what success would look like for her three months from now. As she held back tears, Grace told me that her husband had just lost his job, she was now the sole breadwinner, so success meant making enough money to run her business, pay the mortgage and the personal bills too. She didn't believe it was possible.

But the magic is in the numbers, and the fix, in this case, was simple. You see, Grace hadn't increased her prices for twenty years. She was charging less for her services than a designer straight out of design school. When I asked Grace why she hadn't increased her prices, she admitted it was because she didn't believe she was worth more. That, with a lack of financial knowledge, meant Grace was working sixty-hour weeks for very little, and she'd done that for twenty years!

So, after a lot of work on money beliefs and business money basics, we did a complete pricing overhaul, ensuring that each quote built-in money to cover the cost of doing business, staff wages, a wage for Grace with superannuation included, plus 15% profit. That one increase was the game changer Grace needed to take her business from making less than $100,000 per year to more than half a million a year in turnover, the latter with a 15% profit in the mix, too. And she did that in less than a year!

Grace was shocked that such a significant change could occur in such a small amount of time. And as is often the case, this success encouraged Grace to go on and incorporate as many good financial habits in her business as possible. To this day, she continues to strive for the next level of success in her business, and now she earns a high six-figure salary, and does it working three days a week.

As we go deeper into the twenty-first century, financial literacy is more important than ever, especially for women and young people. There are more women over fifty homeless and living in poverty than ever before. The gender wage gap still exists and gender-biased messaging continues to devalue the choices women make in their day-to-day lives. There are also more women than ever going into small business, so, like it or not, having a handle on the business finances, even if you choose to outsource the finances, is vital!

So, how's your business money knowledge, and what can you do now to change your business and life to reach your unique definition of success?

Here are a few business money basics that might help.

Get educated! Don't be like me and process one thousand hours of BAS returns in an insolvency firm to learn the ropes; instead, do a short course or program like my signature program *Business Money Magnet*, work with a coach, buy a book or jump online and develop a basic understanding of what you need to know to run your business. What are you liable for? What compliance obligations do you need to meet? Know what you can and cannot claim in your taxes; you get the drill.

Open a bank account that's used only for business purposes. Everything you earn goes into that account, and everything you spend goes out. Open two linked savings accounts and start saving for your tax obligations and a rainy day, too.

Have solid systems and processes across the board, especially regarding the business money. Use tech like cloud accounting to save you time and money.

Make the business reports, profit and loss statement and the balance sheet your business BFFs because these numbers will tell you everything you need to know about your business and what you need to do next.

Get proactive! Create a cash flow forecast to anticipate the money lumps and bumps that will inevitably occur in your business. When you understand your cash flow, you'll know when to spend and when to save.

Make a weekly date with yourself to do the numbers! Consider a Money Monday or Finance Friday, put it in the diary and make it non-negotiable. It only needs an hour a week, but it's time dedicated to doing all the business money stuff.

Review your expenses every three months. What do you need to run your business? What are you paying for that you don't use? Are you doubling up on expenses and where can you downgrade to a free version?

Ask for help when you need it! Be sure to call in an accountant, bookkeeper or other finance professional to help. There's no shame in asking for help, even if it's only to understand what to do next.

Perfect your pricing! Regular pricing reviews in your business mean you're always charging enough to cover the cost of doing business, pay yourself a wage, save for a rainy day and have money left over as profit!

Know what success means to you in this season of life and business. Stop comparing yourself to everyone else and strive to reach your unique success goals.

Looking back to 2004, I'm grateful for that $42,000 tax debit. What seemed like a failure then turned out to be a triumphant moment in business because it completely changed my life and business journey. I'll be eternally grateful to the accountant who got it so wrong back then, even though it cost us a lot. That error pushed me to understand the business money and, more importantly, how business success is unique and can change whenever I need it to.

I now know that seasons in business and life will change, and so will you. There will be peaks and troughs in business and life, but your knowledge is constant and ever-growing. Knowledge is powerful because once you have it, no-one can take it away, and it will set you up for success no matter what else is going on in the world.

The knowledge I gained all those years ago helped my business and life success and allowed me to create a multifaceted company. In early 2023, I was able to sell off part of that company, my compliance business, for a profit. Now, I'm fortunate enough to spend my time in financial education, helping other business owners learn the business money foundations that will help them succeed in their business, too. Not bad for someone who didn't do numbers all those years ago, and I wouldn't have it any other way.

So, over to you …

What does success mean to you in this season of life and business?

But before you answer, remember there is always a price for the next level of success. It could be time, energy, money or relationships, but there will always be a price, because no matter who you are, you can't do everything yourself.

However, the price you pay is up to you! At any moment, you can decide what you're prepared to sacrifice to reach your success goals. So be intentional about every decision, and always know it's your business, your life and therefore your choice. When it comes to business the sky's the limit; there are no real constraints, only the ones you impose yourself. Ultimately, it's up to you to decide what success means to you in this season of life and business and what you're prepared to pay to reach the next level of growth.

Justine McLean is a business money mentor and financial educator on a mission to help women in business increase their financial literacy, build solid financial foundations and create profitable and sustainable businesses. Justine has helped countless business owners improve their relationship with money and become the ROI rockstars and money-makers-in-chief of their businesses.

Pricing is Justine's superpower, and her signature program, Business Money Magnet, and new book *Become A Business Money Magnet*, takes the ick out of business finance and helps business owners supercharge their profits.

With thirty years of experience in small business, retail, e-commerce, publishing and finacial services, Justine is sought-after for her practical, tailored and proactive approach to business; clients describe Justine as 'the nice warm hug your business finances need'. A registered BAS agent, host of the *Secrets of Successful Business* podcast, author and ladies finance club ambassador, Justine was named one of the Coach Foundation's Top Female Business Coaches for 2022.

THE BODACIOUS WOMAN

Kabinga Mazaba

A bodacious woman knows the strength of her voice, recognising it as her power, her authenticity. It's her magnetism, the driving force behind her action and the foundation of her legacy. – Kabinga

There exist those women who stand as pillars in our communities, societies and families – icons of confidence and fearlessness. They support other women to win, thrive and have the courage to get up when things seem challenging. I call these women *bodacious*. The name bodacious is a blend of the words 'bold' and 'audacious', it is used to describe someone or something that is remarkably impressive, bold, excellent, admirable or attractive. It describes a confident, self-aware, understanding and loving woman. She is on a path to empower herself and others, overcoming limiting beliefs to achieve greatness.

History has provided us with role models; women defying expectations frequently sparked significant social and cultural changes. For example, Rosa Parks, an American civil rights activist whose refusal to surrender her seat to a white passenger on a segregated bus in Montgomery, Alabama, became a pivotal symbol of the Civil Rights Movement in the sixties. Against all odds, Marie Curie, a Polish-born physicist and chemist, was the first woman to win a Nobel Prize and the only person to win in two different scientific fields (physics and chemistry) for her research on radioactivity. A bodacious woman, Harriet Tubman, an American abolitionist born into slavery, led thirteen rescue missions on the Underground Railroad, freeing around seventy enslaved individuals. A Pakistani activist for female education and the youngest-ever Nobel Prize laureate, Malala Yousafzai, is known for her advocacy in a region where the Taliban had, at times, banned girls from attending school. Last but not least, Emmeline Pankhurst, a British political activist and leader of the British suffragette movement, helped women win the right to vote. These women didn't just change their lives; they transformed their societies. There are both current and historical examples of bold women, worldwide, making significant contributions to improve the world.

Despite its intimidating aspect, venturing out of our comfort zone can be transformative and empowering, especially for women. While the idea that only a tiny percentage of people embrace the unknown might be more symbolic than actual, it highlights the significant impact of those who dare to be different. Each woman's journey beyond her familiar limits is unique, yet every act of bravery shines as an example, inspiring others to venture forth. History is filled with women whose boldness changed their destinies and the world. This challenging journey symbolises the power of embracing the unknown, a step that can open doors to new opportunities and remarkable growth.

A bodacious woman's steps resonate beyond her life, inspiring others and potentially creating a chain reaction of empowerment. Collaboration magnifies this impact, turning individual courage into collective progress. I've embraced boldness and audacity with a desire to fuel a transformative movement in healing past traumatic experiences. This aspiration is anchored in my own life story. Let me draw back the curtain on my early years, unveiling the experiences that shaped my resolve and purpose.

THE DIMMING OF CHILDHOOD JOY

In my early childhood in Zambia, surrounded by a loving yet complex extended family, I experienced both joy and pain. The freedom of my community, while liberating, exposed me to dangers, including sexual and emotional abuse. At six, my innocence was shattered by abuse from my uncle, a trauma repeated at nine by a neighbour. When my parents discovered this, they kept it a secret, failing to seek justice or acknowledge my suffering due to cultural taboos, leaving me burdened with shame and feelings of unworthiness. My life was further marred by the loss of my father in a plane crash at eleven, followed by being publicly disowned by his family immediately after he was put to rest. Following that, my mother's struggles as a single parent left me feeling emotionally abandoned, and her untimely death deepened my sense of loss and pain, significantly shaping my outlook on life.

In my healing from trauma, I learned a profound truth: we don't choose our birth family or foresee life's twists and turns. Life's unpredictability leaves deep scars, with trauma often being overwhelming and stripping away our sense of self and connection. Trauma can be unbearable and debilitating, draining our energy to cope with the memories of abuse, shame and terror. This highlights the need for courageous women to support others in navigating their traumatic experiences.

When you've experienced any kind of abuse, whether it's emotional, sexual, physical or financial, it shakes you to your core. It makes you question everything about who you are and your value. To attain my value, facing my past was not a choice, it was crucial for my inner peace. I had to bravely confront the memories of myself at six, nine and eleven years old – a young girl, with eyes full of tears and a heart burdened with pain. Acknowledging the struggles of my childhood was key to lifting the shadows that lingered into my adult life. Embracing the hurt of that little girl was like walking into a storm, yet it was the path to healing and freedom. This journey, filled with pain and strength, was about reconciling with my past to forge a peaceful, liberated future. I've learned that the past persists until acknowledged and accepted, realising that unaddressed childhood issues can cast long shadows over our adult lives.

During my healing journey, I realised that our resilience is built through trials, shaping us into who we are. These experiences instil a tenacity for life and fill us with compassion and empathy, allowing us to support and guide others through similar challenges. Doing so, we help them grow stronger and transcend their painful past, teaching them that their hearts can still hold gratitude and joy, despite past traumas.

Let me share the essential guiding principles I uncovered during this transformative period; the principles which helped me become a bodacious woman.

KNOW THY WORTH: BELIEF AND ACCEPTANCE!

'Do you want to meet the love of your life? Look in the mirror.'
– Byron Katie

Overcoming your past requires re-evaluating and transforming your identity and self-worth, often shaped by others' limiting beliefs. In redefining my identity, I pondered: What does it take to be an extraordinary woman, and could I achieve that? My aspirations, against my past, felt daunting, almost impossible. The qualities I admired seemed like distant, unreachable stars. Acquiring these traits felt like a fantasy, seemingly exclusive to those born in more nurturing environments.

Realising your worth is a profoundly personal journey, independent of others' opinions. It involves recognising your value and finding the answers within yourself. Acknowledging your worth enables you to make the most of life's opportunities and is essential for mental wellbeing. 'Know thy worth: belief and acceptance' emphasises understanding your inherent value, self-belief and acceptance of your strengths and flaws. This self-recognition is crucial in developing a positive self-image and overall wellbeing.

Emulating luminaries like Rosa Parks and Marie Curie means embodying their spirit of courage, conviction and self-belief, rather than replicating their achievements. It involves the bravery to challenge norms, stand by your beliefs and the resilience to overcome adversity. This journey requires a commitment to continuous learning and growth, using experiences as opportunities to evolve. It's about making an empathetic impact and driving positive change in the world while being true to yourself. Your unique path, informed by their qualities but distinctly yours, can lead to inspiring heights. By adhering to these principles, your journey can be impactful, creating a legacy that reflects your voice and vision.

KICK OUT YOUR LIMITING BELIEFS; CREATE THE LIFE YOU WANT!

> *'Taking responsibility for your beliefs and judgements gives you the power to change them.'* – Byron Katie

Women on the brink of change must eliminate limiting beliefs. These beliefs act as powerful limiters, subtly directing our lives and acting as shackles on potential. They insidiously undermine our abilities, creating glass ceilings rather than open skies and defining the boundaries of our potential, often within self-imposed limits. These beliefs influence our thoughts, actions and emotions, shaping our reality. My transformative journey began by recognising the limiting beliefs rooted in my childhood. Confronting these beliefs, intertwined with emotional baggage and past experiences, was the first step in rewriting my story and creating the life I desired. Unwavering determination, commitment and consistency were essential to instil new, empowering beliefs in my life. Remember, every breakthrough in history has stemmed from a radical belief shift – a positive outlook on life and the future, affirming that individually and collectively, we are powerful, resourceful and limitless, capable of living fulfilling and abundant lives.

Overcoming limiting beliefs starts with owning them; acknowledging our past limiting beliefs and judgements empowers us to transform them. The bodacious woman does not merely question, she shatters these invisible barriers through a gradual and sometimes dramatic change process through habit formation. She harnesses these beliefs as the fuel for her transformative journey, turning each doubt into a stepping stone towards empowerment. She recognises that her struggle against limiting beliefs is not a solitary fight. It's a beacon of hope for those still entangled in the web of self-doubt. She becomes a mentor, a guide, leading by example and showing that the shackles of limiting beliefs can be forged into tools of liberation and growth.

By challenging her constraints, she opens doors for others, creating a domino effect of empowerment. Her journey becomes a shared narrative, a collective rising against the odds. This is the heart of the Badious Woman's legacy – using her battles against limiting beliefs not just as personal victories, but as powerful narratives to ignite change, inspire action and pave the way for a world where the potential is not curbed by the invisible chains of doubt, but is celebrated and nurtured into fruition. She is driven to serve, not by competing with others, but by collaborating with like-minded women who help others live better lives.

ELEVATE THE SOUL OF MIND; ALIGN YOUR LIFE WITH CORE VALUES!

Every thought in our mind is a seed.

The critical piece of my life's puzzle was always my mind. I needed to revise my mindset to realise my dreams, profoundly shedding limiting beliefs and negativity. Actively changing my thoughts to focus on possibilities, courage and self-belief, I transformed my outlook and life, turning my mind from a barrier into a source of strength and guidance towards success and fulfilment.

To balance and elevate my mind, I recognised the importance of framing it with values. Like a lighthouse, these values guided me, helping me find a path to happiness and tranquillity. They provided clarity and purpose, becoming a personal compass for making decisions that deeply resonated with who I am. This alignment with my core values transformed every action into a step towards a meaningful life, leading to success, fulfilment and living a life that was authentically mine.

The 'soul of the mind' metaphorically represents our cognitive and emotional core, the essence of our consciousness and identity. It emphasises the depth of our intellectual and emotional capacities, portraying the mind as more than just a part of existence but as a masterful conductor of our life's journey. This concept elevates our understanding of the mind's transformative power, guiding us towards a purposeful destination.

Every thought we cultivate in our minds can reshape our values and empower us to make a significant difference in the lives of others.

UNLEASHING CREATIVE POWER

In creativity, we don't just think outside the box but redefine it.

Creativity plays a crucial role in forging the path of a bodacious woman on a journey towards making a difference for herself and others. This creative force is not merely about generating new ideas but tapping into our inner reservoir of imagination to reshape, redefine and add vibrancy to the world around us. Bodacious women embrace this power, viewing challenges not as obstacles but as canvases for innovation. They use their unique perspectives and insights to bring about change in personal lives, communities or beyond. This creative power is a beacon that guides them toward personal fulfilment and lights the way for others, inspiring collective growth and progress.

By unleashing our creative potential, we step into a realm where we are not just participants in our stories but the compelling authors of an ever-evolving narrative of empowerment and transformation. I used my creative power to write a book.

THE CALL FOR RESILIENCE

Every moment in life is a journey; how we travel it is our choice.

Life doesn't discriminate in its trials, big or small, and everyone faces unique battles. These experiences, from triumphs to adversities, shape us and present a choice: to endure our fate or actively shape our story passively. Embracing life's unpredictable journey, filled with transformative experiences, encourages us to find meaning in every challenge. Resilience is key; it's not just about recovery but fully embracing life's complexity. Our response to adversity defines us, offering daily choices to either be overwhelmed or to rise stronger. This call for resilience is more than survival, it's a testament to our spirit's capacity to overcome obstacles. By accepting this journey, we learn to find joy and strength in adversity by maintaining a balanced perspective, turning daunting challenges into stepping stones towards a more prosperous, more fulfilling life.

Resilience is a bodacious woman's most exquisite armour, turning life's challenges into stepping stones for growth. Her grace in adversity fuels her indomitable spirit to emerge stronger and reshape life with courage and steadfast determination.

SEAL OF SELF-ACCEPTANCE: REINVENT AND EMPOWER YOURSELF

'Each of us has that right, that possibility, to invent ourselves daily. If a person does not invent herself, she will be invented. So, to be bodacious enough to invent ourselves is wise.' – Maya Angelou

For too long, I lived with a borrowed identity. I realised that self-acceptance is crucial for authenticity, and without it, a false self may take over, leading to a life filled with uncertainty and 'why' questions. Embracing it anchors our purpose and empowers us to impact and inspire others positively. Maya Angelou's words highlight the importance of self-creation through self-acceptance. She encourages us to reinvent ourselves daily, shaping our identity rather than being moulded by external forces. This isn't about superficial changes, but a courageous journey of self-discovery and growth, aligning with our true nature. It involves embracing our evolving selves and reflecting on our core values and aspirations. This ongoing process of self-acceptance and reinvention allows us to live authentically, ensuring our actions and choices truly represent us.

Embracing every facet of who you are is the key to a life rich in contentment and joy. Embrace the audacious woman within by painting a vision that propels you forward. As you navigate the seas of possibility, arm yourself bravely and let faith be the wind in your sails. Execution is your rudder; steer with intention and let curiosity chart your course. Equip your mind with knowledge and wisdom for the journey ahead. Surround yourself with people whose greatness reflects your aspirations. And should you stumble, rise with the invaluable treasure of lessons learned, weaving them into the fabric of your ever-evolving story. Shine on, bodacious woman, for your path is one of impact and inspiration.

If you admit it, you can change; if you confront it, you can heal. – Kabinga

Kabinga C Mazaba, originally from Zambia, is a rising literary talent and a dedicated mental health expert specialising in trauma recovery. Her journey, marked by overcoming childhood trauma, epitomises the extraordinary strength of the human spirit. As a transformation and mindset coach, keynote international speaker and author, Kabinga's work, especially her Amazon number-one bestselling book *C.O.N.F.R.O.N.T: Reclaim Your Life*, is a guiding light for those on their paths to healing and transformation.

With deep insights into the human psyche, Kabinga creates a nurturing space for self-realisation amidst life's complexities. Her coaching helps clients navigate their mental landscapes, moving from self-doubt to clarity and authentic self-awareness. On stage, Kabinga captivates audiences with her magnetic presence, sharing stories of resilience that inspire and act as catalysts for personal change. Her blend of compassion and strength positions her as a bridge-builder, guiding people from their past selves to their full potential.

In her relentless pursuit of knowledge, Kabinga is actively working towards a degree in counselling, underscoring her deep commitment to aiding individuals in overcoming challenges, finding peace after trauma, and embarking on journeys of profound personal growth. Kabinga's philosophy, 'life is a journey, embrace uncertainty', reflects her belief in the power of resilience and adaptability. This principle infuses her personal and professional endeavours with purpose and determination, guiding her in making impactful contributions to the mental health field.

Balancing her professional achievements, Kabinga is a nurturing mother of three and a loving wife, exemplifying her belief in harmonising career aspirations with family life. Her story is not just about personal triumph but also about empowering others through empathy and compassion. Her WHY for her career extends beyond her narrative, fuelled by an unwavering desire to support others in their healing, ensuring everyone can find happiness and live authentically.

Her book, *C.O.N.F.R.O.N. T: Reclaim Your Life,* is more than a memoir of Kabinga's journey through trauma; it's a testament to human resilience. Through sharing her experiences, she aims to offer hope and inspiration to those lost in the shadows, providing the courage needed to confront their challenges and reclaim their lives. Kabinga C Mazaba is a role model for personal growth, symbolising the potential to rise from adversity and inspire a world needing hope and understanding. With Kabinga, inspiration isn't just a word; it's an experience that will elevate you towards your envisioned life.

Website: kabingamazaba.com
Facebook: facebook.com/kabingamazaba
Instagram: instagram.com/kabingamazaba
LinkedIn: linkedin.com/in/kabingamazaba

BECOMING UNBROKEN

HOW BREAKING MY SILENCE TAUGHT ME THAT THE VALUE OF MY WORDS ISN'T FOUND IN THE SIZE OF MY AUDIENCE

Kate Fisher

In April 2023, I found myself in London, standing with a microphone, in front of the most phenomenal women at the Women Changing the World Global Summit. I was sharing the work I do in blood donation advocacy and at that moment, I understood that my work had a place on an international stage. The need for blood and blood donors holds equal value all over the world.

As I stood sharing information about the persistent and critical nature of blood shortages, I felt a strength and sense of identity I hadn't felt in many years. It was like catching up with an old friend from a previous chapter in my life. One with whom I had lost touch and did not expect to ever see again in this season of my life. I embraced a new aspect of purpose in my life, and it was so refreshing to stand in front of sets of fresh eyes who had no idea how broken I had been, and that only recently, I had not expected to be in a position where my passion for the betterment of health and social outcomes could be utilised ever again. I thought I had lost my voice and my worth.

In 2016, at the age of thirty-two, I suffered an injury birthing our daughter that would result in my invalidity retirement from my public service career. It was deemed I would never again be able to do my job, and at the time, my interpretation of that was that I would no longer contribute to my family financially. I felt my years of undergraduate and postgraduate study were redundant, and I was no longer able to make positive contributions to society or our local community. While elements of all of those things are still true to this day, it's been such a triumph to find my new identity. I wonder how different my case would be assessed if it happened now, in the post-COVID world, where it is broadly assumed that the traditional nine-to-five, forty-hour work week, in an office setting, will never return.

By 2019, my time was devoted to a much more demanding career than my previous one and it was the greatest honour of my life. I became not just a full-time parent but also a carer. The distinction came for me when I realised that 'mothering' was what I was able to do in my spare time, and the mental load of motherhood is brutal when raising four children, three of those who are living, and all of whom have chronic health conditions, alongside physical and neuro-developmental disabilities.

One of the best and easiest choices I ever made was marrying my amazing husband, Geoff, who regularly reminds me that he 'married all of me'. For us, that meant starting IVF before we were even married. Knowing that my chances of conceiving and maintaining pregnancies were slim, he chose me anyway. We've always said that our wedding was the day we chose to celebrate the commitment we'd made to each other long ago, with the people we love the most in the world. Our greatest joy was announcing during the ceremony that our first baby, a boy we called Thomas, was kicking away in my belly! What we couldn't have known was how many times we would need to keep choosing each other, loving and trusting each other, in the face of adversity. Our belief that the most horrific experience of our lives (knowing one of our identical twin boys was dying, enduring the rest of that pregnancy and then birthing both boys), was challenged by the experience of being told our youngest child, Marleigh, was going to die.

At the age of three, Marleigh started suffering terrifying seizures. The longest was a thirty-nine-hour status epilepticus seizure which required an airlift to a specialised paediatric intensive care unit (PICU). She was intubated and placed into an induced coma. We didn't know if she would survive, and despite eight months of testing, consults with specialists all over the world, as well as samples of Marleigh's cerebral spinal fluid being taken via lumbar puncture and sent to Los Angeles and Berlin, we seemed no closer to an answer about why medication-resistant seizures continued to ravage our little girl's brain.

It was during the first admission to PICU (we would become regulars in the year that followed) that I heard about a condition called autoimmune encephalitis and the incredible power of something called intravenous immunoglobulin infusion (IVIG) which is made from donated human blood and plasma. I swiftly gave my consent for her to try the treatment and for the first time we had some good news. We were closer to a formal diagnosis and had a treatment protocol that worked for Marleigh. I am still astounded that no amount of medicine or science could help our girl, but the kindness of Australian plasma donors saved her life. While I didn't recognise it at the time, this was where the first seed of inspiration was planted for the blood donation advocacy movement I would go on to create.

Marleigh's eventual diagnosis was seronegative paediatric autoimmune encephalitis. A condition that has no cure, however treatment is possible with IVIG, which is a broad spectrum of antibodies created from donated human plasma. For Marleigh, this treatment has been lifesaving when she has an acute relapse and life-preserving for every infusion in-between. She is now eight years old and in remission. Through extensive rehabilitation, she is no longer using a speech device or her wheelchair. She is, however, flanked by her seizure response service dog, Paddy – a chocolate Labrador who alerts us to seizures hours before they arrive and has spent countless hours supporting her inside hospital rooms.

When Marleigh was at her sickest, she was having IVIG every two weeks, for nineteen months. Unfortunately, this was also at the height of the COVID-19 pandemic when Australia experienced critical blood shortages. If we spaced her treatments longer than fourteen days apart, Marleigh would have life-threatening seizures. So as a family, we were stuck in a cycle of knowing that we could preserve Marleigh's life for up to two weeks at a time and living in hope that enough Australians donated plasma to ensure there was enough available for her treatment. This was the beginning of my understanding of the precarious nature of the blood supply in Australia and that blood donors don't just keep people alive, they keep families together. For us, this was keeping a daughter with her parents and a little sister with her big brothers.

In the lead-up to the first anniversary of Marleigh's first IVIG, I wanted to celebrate her year of survival. I had seen the power of telling Marleigh's story in engaging our family and friends as blood donors. I put a call out through my personal social media accounts, hoping to recruit one hundred donors in one hundred days for the Milkshakes for Marleigh Lifeblood team. The concept was that when you donate blood, you are often offered a milkshake afterwards – hence having a Milkshake for Marleigh. The response I received was astounding. Over three hundred donations were made in Marleigh's name, made up of whole blood, platelet and plasma donations, from every state and territory in Australia. If this was the impact I could have sharing Marleigh's story with a very modest social media campaign, what if I created a way to tell the stories of many blood recipients and their loved ones?

As I was dreaming of how to expand my idea, Marleigh had an acute autoimmune encephalitis relapse. For the third time in eleven months, an emergency helicopter was sent to retrieve Marleigh from Canberra to The Sydney Children's Hospital. Due to COVID-19 regulations, only one parent could be bedside with her in PICU. I'm so grateful that Geoff selflessly gifted me that time with her. It meant I was the one who had the terrifying conversation with the emergency medicine doctor when he informed me that Marleigh was displaying the signs of COVID-19 and that she needed to be placed into an insolation room. It would take twenty-four to thirty-six hours for the results of the two negative tests that were required for her to be released from isolation, but the doctors didn't expect her to survive for very long. As Geoff and I had been in contact with Marleigh, and she was considered potentially COVID-19 positive, we were no longer allowed on hospital grounds. The only kindness that could be offered was giving me ten minutes to say goodbye to her as they made the preparations for transfer. Despite the abundant personal protective equipment (PPE), very few medical staff in the PICU that day could hide their tears at the injustice. I'm not sure if it was shock or adrenalin, but I chose not to waste a second of that ten minutes arguing.

What would you say or do if you only had ten minutes left with your precious child? I'm still in awe of the woman I became in those ten minutes. I video-called Geoff, informing him that he needed to say goodbye to his little girl and tell her anything that was left unsaid. I wrote her a letter from her brothers and recorded myself reading her a bedtime story. If she was to die, I told the nurses I wanted them to make it feel as much as possible like I was reading her a story while she was drifting off to sleep. Ever so slightly masking the fact that she would be in a hospital isolation room alone but surrounded by strangers in full PPE. Finally, as they were preparing to wheel her away from me, I stood at the head of her bed and let my tears fall – 'happy tears', as Marleigh calls them – and I did the most unexpected thing; I told her that she didn't have to fight anymore, that I loved her with my whole heart, and that there was no greater love than the one we shared. I said she couldn't bring more joy to the world in the next forty years than she has in the last four. I reminded her that when she got to the other side, she was to look for the boy who looked just like her big brother, Campbell, as his identical twin Benjamin would be waiting there for her, and to stay with him until Mummy got there. I've listened back to that 'bedtime story' recording, and while in the moment it felt like the purest form of love, what I can hear is the beeping of machines, screeching of alarms and the rhythmic hum of the ventilator that was causing Marleigh's chest to robotically rise and fall, which in the end was very important, as Marleigh had developed septic pneumonia, secondary to intubation which can manifest with symptoms just like COVID-19. With the sepsis came a whole new fight for her life, but against the odds she made it through, again, with the assistance of blood products.

It was twenty-eight hours and thirty-five minutes before I saw Marleigh again, and it was hard to believe that she could look worse than when I'd said goodbye to her earlier. Remarkably, she was still hanging on to life. It was another five days before she was brought out of the coma and then slowly able to breathe on her own. When she was finally conscious, she didn't recognise me or Geoff. We weren't sure how severe her brain injury was and if she would ever walk or talk again. My greatest fear wasn't that she would die, but that she would die alone. It was a cruelty that I couldn't bear and every medical professional, psychologist or social worker I told reassured me that she was so heavily medicated, she would never remember any of that time. But as she regained her speech and spent time with the phenomenal child-centred play therapist, she expressed that she floated up out of her bed and through the window in the roof to look for me. That's where she found the rainbows, and the rainbows took her back to her mummy.

Whether it be kissing Marleigh's head in that tiny hospital room or standing in front of thousands of people talking about persistent critical blood shortages in Australia and around the world, my voice has power. Through my blood donation advocacy work, I have become a change-maker, developing a creative solution to a social problem, by creating a movement when those who have needed blood (and their loved ones) tell their stories to thank their donors and encourage new ones. For some, this is survival. For others, it's improving quality of life, providing treatment options or keeping someone alive just long enough to say goodbye to the people they love. Blood donors give the gift of time.

When I found myself standing with that microphone at the Women Changing the World Summit in April 2023, nobody could have known that due to the post-obstetric pudendal neuralgia I suffered during my birth injury, that I was suffering from urinary incontinence. The vaginal

Valium I'd used to enable me to endure the thirty hours of travel to get from Brisbane, Queensland, to London, England, is a muscle relaxant and does have some unfortunate side effects. I weighed more than I ever have, due to my inability to exercise due to my injury, and eating only what was available in the parents' kitchen on children's hospital wards (I can confirm it is possible to sustain life for over a year almost exclusively on Vegemite on toast and coffee!), but none of these physical characteristics mattered at all that day. When you've been to the brink with someone you love that much, you realise that the way we look has so little to do with the mark we leave on this world. My words were much more powerful than that! It was the last time I let my physical limitations, or my appearance, silence me.

I could no longer stay silent when I had a vision that could affect social change and increase blood donations around the world, and I learned quickly that the size of my audience doesn't change the value of my words. Whether it be in the early episodes of my podcast, when my audience was tiny, or to the thousands I now address, I will always know some of the most powerful words I've ever spoken were to an audience of one: when I said what I thought was my *goodbye* to Marleigh.

A dear friend suggested to me when describing my work that, 'When you make something from the heart, when you tell your truth and it lands, that's profound and that's success.' Marleigh will be dependent on blood donors for life and if I've done my job properly then she will always have what she needs.

KATE FISHER

Kate Fisher is an award-winning Australian storyteller and change-maker. She is well-known as Australia's fiercest blood donation advocate.

Kate is the founder of Milkshakes for Marleigh; host and executive producer of the *Milkshakes for Marleigh* podcast and author of the *Milkshakes for Marleigh* book.

She has a daughter who is dependent on blood products to survive so she is on a mission to end persistent critical blood shortages in Australia and around the world.

LESSONS I HAVE LEARNT ALONG THE WAY

Laura Goldberg

When I embarked on the journey of writing this chapter, I was hoping to find one pivotal moment that would define how I became a *woman making a difference,* but truthfully, there was not just one moment, but rather a series of small lessons along the journey that have made the most impact and formed who I am. I'm here to share some of the most important lessons I've learnt on my way to truly making a difference in the world.

THE IMPORTANCE OF POSITIVE ROLE MODELS

I grew up in Johannesburg, South Africa; a big, vast city in Africa. I was born during apartheid, something that fortunately didn't affect me directly, but affected many people around me, and as a result taught me so much about equality and the importance of tolerance, charity and compassion. My parents worked hard to provide my brothers and me with the best education and life. We were somewhat sheltered from life's hardships and had what can only be described as an idyllic childhood. I was so lucky to be surrounded by my extended family, including both sets of grandparents and a myriad of aunties, uncles, cousins and second cousins. Looking back on my childhood, I was influenced by the many incredible women I was lucky to have around me.

My maternal grandmother, who travelled across the globe at thirty years old to marry the love of her life and then went on to raise six exceptional humans, while running a business and caring for her husband as he battled cancer.

My paternal grandmother also left her home in Madeira with three children in tow to travel to South Africa so my grandfather could fulfil his dreams. She went to South Africa without knowing a word of English and managed to forge an amazing life for herself, surrounded by her church and the multiple friends she made along the way.

My mother, who is the definition of class and tolerance, has taught me everything I know about being a mother, leader, role model and boss.

Most of my aunts and cousins – they either worked for themselves or for other family members.

I had no idea that this was not the norm, and these strong independent women taught me that I did not have to be defined by the expectations that come with having a strict Portuguese upbringing. In fact, we can use this to our advantage, and anything is possible.

I wasn't the best student, but nor was I the worst, and looking back attending an all-girls school, my teachers certainly provided me with exposure to some great women. I can sometimes hear my teachers' voices in my head, mostly telling me to stop talking, which is funny since most of my work involves talking. The one stand-out feature of all of these teachers is that we were always told we could become whatever we wanted, without restriction.

The beauty of being able to write this chapter is that I am able to go back and reflect on how important these women were in shaping the leader and role model I hope I am today.

I am so lucky to have been surrounded by so many amazing women from my childhood, and how I am now able to see other women as true collaborators, not competition. Now, as I grow older, I am drawn to other women who inspire me and raise me up, much like the amazing women who shaped my childhood.

THE IMPORTANCE OF PARTNERSHIP

How many times have we been told we can *have it all?* Be the change-maker, raise the kids, be the best friend, run a business, stay fit, run a household etc. etc. etc. How boring!

WOMEN MAKING A DIFFERENCE

I think we have to accept that, as women, we can be many things at the same time, but we can't be everything to everyone at the same time. We should be able to say *no*, to decide who we see and who we choose to spend our time with. That's where the strength of partnerships comes in. Some of us are fortunate to have partners who support us and truly share in the daily grinds of life, but I have learned over the years that, unless you ask for help, no-one will come running to save you. So, ask for help, reach out – actually physically *ask* for help. I see so much strength in asking, because when we share our burdens, we become stronger as a society.

Growing up in South Africa, we had a full-time live-in nanny which allowed my mum to go about building her business. She also had family help, which meant that my cousins and I spent a lot of time together! Another example of partnerships. My cousins became partners in our lives, and we have formed bonds that can never be broken.

These days, I'm usually the mum who calls other mums to help me, or more often than not, my mother-in-law. But I don't think that makes me a bad parent, it just means I have some great partners who allow me to be a woman who can make a difference. I am also the mother who puts her hand up *first* to help, if I can.

The ultimate partnership in my life is my husband; the one person who cheers me on the loudest, who encourages me when I think I can't do something, and who picks up the slack when I need to write a chapter in a book. We are both partners in business and in our everyday lives.

THE IMPORTANCE OF HAVING FAITH

Throughout my life I have been surrounded by people of great faith. I have often struggled with it, but as I get older I have become more receptive to the idea of faith and belief. During one of the most challenging times in my life, I was able to lean on my faith, and it got me through. In 2021, the hardest year of my life, I nearly lost my mother to COVID. She was very sick on the other side of the globe, and I needed to get to her. Somehow, I managed to get an exemption to get to South Africa and see her, in what we believed would be her last days. I learnt the true meaning of hope and faith in that time. But I also believe that, to change the world, we need to have faith in ourselves; faith that we can overcome obstacles, face adversity and come out triumphant on the other side.

In order to have faith in yourself, you must find someone who has faith in you first. I am so lucky that I am surrounded by people who have faith in me, even when I don't always have the answers. And sometimes the people who believe in you are the people you least expect – the lady down the road, the neighbour, the colleague or even your own children.

THE IMPORTANCE OF MINDSET

Mindset is the buzzword of our times, but probably the single most important factor in changing your life and the lives of people around you. In 2020, I was invited to a conference for women about women in business. I really thought I was out of my league, but it got me thinking. If someone thought I was special enough to be invited, then I must have something to offer. I changed my mindset from someone who didn't believe in her value, to someone who was just as important as every other woman in the room. This small shift in thinking has changed my life. I started to read more, challenge myself and truly believe that I could change the world in some way.

The change of mindset has opened so many doors for me. I encourage anyone to listen to the teachings of Jay Shetty, Jim Kwik, Barbara and Allan Pease, just to name a few. Of course, there are times when stuff gets me down and I go back into victim mentality, but every morning I listen to a podcast on mindset and I reprogram my brain. This takes work and perseverance, but a small change to your thinking can open so many doors.

I wish that mindset training had been available to me during my early career, but I now try to teach my children about changing their mindset.

And through a small change in mindset, we are able to manifest some amazing things. Mindset training enables us to be receptive to small ideas, new thought patterns and, more importantly, new experiences. Saying yes and changing my mindset, I was able to go to London and Paris where I shared some of my entrepreneurial experiences, met some amazing women and got completely out of my comfort zone.

The most powerful mindsets are those of growth, change and self-improvement, believing you have the ability to grow will truly allow you to achieve things you didn't think possible.

THE IMPORTANCE OF FRIENDSHIP

We are so often taught that other women around us are 'competition', but I don't believe that at all. I believe we can learn from even our closest competitor. Once we open our hearts to the notion that there is enough space in the world for every single human to shine, then truly great things happen. Imagine a world where we all work together and allow ourselves to be our most beautiful authentic selves?

During my schooling, I attended an all-girls school. A convent which, in the eighties in the midst of apartheid South Africa, allowed girls of all faiths and colours. I was exposed to girls from a variety of different cultures and at the time, I don't think we were aware of how lucky we were not to be segregated. The friendships I formed were strong and deep, and I'm fortunate enough to still be friends with some of those dynamic women today. Friendship comes in all shapes and forms, and when you find the people who align with your values, you are truly able to shine.

These past few years have been an amazing learning curve and I have embraced different friendships from men and women from all walks of life. But finding your tribe, the people around you that cheer you on, believe in you and pick you up when you think you can't go any further, these are the people who allow you and help you to become a woman who can truly change the world. My closest confidants are not the people

I see every day, but rather, those who see my value and encourage me to *be more* and *do more*. Alone we are strong, but together we are stronger. This is also the spirit of ubuntu (I am what I am because of who we all are); an African term embraced by many sporting teams, including my beloved Springboks.

Which brings me to my last and probably the most important lessons of all:

THE IMPORTANCE OF SELF-CARE AND GRATITUDE

Anyone who knows me will know that five to six days a week, you'll find me at the gym or doing some form of exercise. This is non-negotiable for me; something that is mine and mine alone. It is the time of day when I give 100% to myself. It can be at the gym, on a powerwalk, boxing, strength training or even something as simple as a stroll with the dog.

This part of my day allows me to sit with gratitude for the body I have, even with its imperfections. It reminds me how lucky I am to be alive and to be able to move freely without pain. During the long dark months when my mother was in hospital, I was still able to get to the gym every day and this small simple action helped my mental health significantly. Moving your body is an act of self-love and one I firmly believe in. There have been many moments when I have felt lost, alone and without direction, but once I release through feel-good hormones, I'm ready to tackle the next goal! What a privilege to be alive.

My husband and I walk often; we try for at least once a week. We call this our 'work walks'. We strategise and talk about our goals and how we will achieve them. We also try to embrace the beauty around us. By allowing ourselves to be outside away from any office – or in our case, restaurant – we are able to see things from a different perspective. And how blessed are we to live in such a beautiful country that allows us the freedom to walk unhindered.

Running a business is stressful at the best of times as any small business owner will testify, but I am grateful for the opportunities that come with it. The business has allowed me the freedom to pursue other interests and goals and has given me the space to become a business leader, philanthropist and volunteer. I continue to be involved in various projects that strive to empower women from all walks of life, to be charitable and offer my time to mentor and help girls and women. I am able to inspire the next generation of hospitality owners, and perhaps, offer some small words of wisdom that can only come from experience. And perhaps, most importantly, I am able to teach my children that you don't have to be the greatest at any given thing to make a difference in the world, that making a difference can be as simple as helping one person and inspiring them to improve themselves. These small lessons have helped me and made me realise how I am making a difference, one small step at a time.

LAURA GOLDBERG

I'm Laura Goldberg, BA Psych (Hons) & BComm in Marketing. At forty-six, I'm a proud mother of two wonderful children, Ethan and Gia. Originally from Johannesburg, South Africa, my family heritage is Portuguese. After a brief stint on a tennis scholarship in the US, I returned home to pursue two degrees at the University of South Africa. During this time, I took over my parents' leather and luggage business, witnessing significant growth while studying through correspondence. In 2002, I immigrated to Australia, initially working for international clothing brands before following my passion for personal training, a journey that spanned ten years.

Today, I am the co-owner of Hurricane's Grill Restaurants alongside my husband Craig, who founded the brand in 1994. Our South African/Australian style steakhouse has expanded to three restaurants in Sydney (Brighton Le Sands, Circular Quay and Castle Hill) and franchised locations in Bankstown and Pyrmont. We've also ventured into Dubai, Indonesia and China, with exciting plans for more growth. Additionally, we are proud partners in our hospitality company, C & L Hospitality Group. Recently, I launched my new co-brand, The Sausage Sizzle Company, providing catering services for schools, charities and BBQ events. I am also the director of a South African leather brand called Jekyll and Hide.

Our Circular Quay restaurant has won multiple awards, including the Australian Small Business Champion award and City of Sydney local business award. Personally, I have been honoured as a finalist for Business Person of the Year in Bayside, Sydney City and St George councils. I've also been a finalist in the Australian Women's Small Business Champion Awards for two years running and finalist for five categories of AusMumpreneur Awards. One of my proudest moments, however, was being named Volunteer of the Year for Easts Rugby Club.

Beyond business, I am passionate about empowering girls and women. I mentor young women and recently participated in the Inspire Her conference in Sydney in collaboration with Edutech Australia. In March 2023, I had the opportunity to join a female founders' tour to London and Paris, where I was featured on two international panels discussing my entrepreneurial journey. As a co-author of the Amazon bestselling and multiple-award-winning book, *Curiosity Killed the 9-5*, I am committed to sharing insights and inspiring others.

When I'm not working, I actively engage in various charities and volunteer my time, whether it's supporting my kids' parents' associations or grilling behind the BBQ at school and rugby club fundraisers. Six days of the week you will find me in the gym or outdoors exercising my body and mind.

UNCOMPLICATING EMPATHY

A GUIDE TO MAKING A DIFFERENCE

Leanne Butterworth

> *"Life is really simple, but we insist on making it complicated."*
> **Confucius**

In September 2023, I was excited and honoured to be a guest at the Social Impact in the Regions Conference in Coffs Harbour, Australia. There, the brilliant environmental activist, Rebel Black, described the powerful difference between the words *complex* and *complicated*. Her passion for biodiversity drove her desire to understand how we tend to create convoluted solutions to problems within complex systems, often preventing us from making positive change.

As Black guided us through her contrasting definitions, she suggested that something complex is intricate and elaborate with a multitude of connected parts; whereas something complicated is inherently confusing and difficult to analyse or explain.

As Black spoke, I thought about how this comparison might apply to my favourite topic - empathy; to be more precise, healthy empathy. Humans are extraordinarily multifaceted and nuanced creatures. On any given day, we are estimated to have over six thousand thoughts and over four hundred emotional experiences. Psychologist Robert Plutchik has suggested that humans may possess a staggering thirty-four thousand different emotions. In my experience, however, many of us can only name about five without thinking about it too much. Underlying this human intricacy, we each have our own unique genetics, experiences, biases, likes, dislikes, expectations, abilities, strengths, and so on. Humans are indeed *complex*.

When it comes to empathy, we know it's something we're supposed to aspire to do or be, but if I asked you now to write down your definition, what would you write? You might jot down something about putting yourself in someone else's shoes or feeling what someone else feels - which might be positive or repellent. Empathy is a concept that we think is simple, until we tie ourselves in knots trying to define it. We may think we know what it is but we kind of don't at the same time. It feels *complicated*.

And it makes perfect sense that empathy is hard to pin down. Even the *origin* of the word isn't straight forward. According to historian Susan Lanzoni, the word empathy only appeared in our language in the early 1900's and is derived from the Greek *empatheia*, from em "in" + pathos "feeling". The word also follows from the German word *Einfühlung* which similarly means "in-feeling", although it primarily related to objects of art and nature.

Today's broad understanding of empathy includes the related concepts of sympathy, compassion, pity, emotional sensing and taking on someone else's perspective. No wonder we're confused. I've also heard the perpetual misguided statements of:

- "You're either born with it, or you're not"
- "Empathy is give, give, give"
- "Empathy doesn't belong at work"
- "Empathy is a weakness"
- "I don't have time for empathy"
- "Empathy leads to burnout"

What do each of these statements have in common? Avoidance. As humans, when we don't understand something, we tend to avoid it. It feels easier that way. We avoid emotionally connecting with others, so we don't have to experience that uncomfortable feeling of emotional vulnerability. We avoid empathy to alleviate the pressure we put on ourselves to know *exactly* the right thing to do or say to make things better, thereby avoiding the risk of rejection or humiliation. We get to stay infallible. Simple.

And I get it. Perfectionism is my default setting. My mother tells me that when I was in primary school, if I thought there was a chance I was going to get something wrong on my homework, I didn't even attempt the question. I thought I had to be right and "perfect" to be valuable. This defence mechanism aimed to shield me from failure, when in truth, it weakened my ability to connect with others.

However, people don't emotionally connect with perfection, they connect with our humanity, our imperfections and our vulnerability. For me, empathy is something I've made an effort to learn, and I discovered that it *can* be learned. My perfectionism led me down the path of post-natal depression but also, ultimately, unlocked my understanding of empathy.

When my kids were small, I struggled. I found that motherhood challenged my desire for perfectionism by the hour. I was lonely and angry and every day I thought of "driving off into the sunset." I wanted out. I remember crying on my kitchen floor with my two confused little toddlers rubbing my back saying they were sorry and asking how to make things better. I felt isolated, like I had control over nothing.

At the same time, the adults around me had the best intentions when they said things like, "the days are long, the years are short", "cherish these moments", "we all got through it", and "medication comes in two varieties - red and white (wine)". But all of these platitudes made me feel worse. More alone. Disconnected. Misunderstood.

When my youngest child turned three, we were at her annual development check when the doctor asked how I was.

"I'm fine." I casually dismissed the question.

"No," she pressed, "really, Leanne. How are *you*?"

I laughed and blurted out, "well I'm stressed from the moment I open my eyes to the moment I close them. Even then, I'm not sleeping and I'm a seething ball of rage. You know, yay for motherhood, huh?"

She had small children too, so I knew she'd get it, but she caught me off guard with, "Leanne, this is bigger than you think it is. Let's see what's going on." Our doctor was the first person who actually *saw me*. She listened, she understood and she supported me.

Eventually it became clear that I had late-diagnosed post-natal depression which, of course, terrified my inner perfectionist. Initially, I felt like a failure wondering what I did wrong, but I had a doctor who normalised my experience and guided me through medication and therapy. To this day, I'm convinced that my doctor's empathy saved my life.

In the years since my diagnosis, I have sought to understand what it was about my doctor's response that was so impactful, and found myself wrestling with the question of empathy. Since empathy is a relatively new concept, a single definition is yet to exist and there are researchers all over the world exploring its social, physical, cognitive and neuroscientific foundations. The definition I developed, is based on the work of American emotional intelligence gurus Daniel Goleman and Paul Ekman. They describe empathy as having three types - emotional (feeling), cognitive (thinking) and compassionate (doing), which I have expanded into an understanding of healthy empathy.

Emotional empathy tends to be the most familiar - feeling the feelings that belong to other people. It's also called emotional contagion, when we *catch* the feelings of others. For example, we might feel anxious when a friend seems anxious. Emotional empathy is the one that can be uncomfortable if we don't want to feel more than we already do. Feeling what others feel, however, is part of being human and builds relationships. If we don't have good emotional boundaries, however, and repeatedly internalise others' emotions, we can become overwhelmed. We may experience emotional burn out, negatively affecting our health and our relationships. As a coping mechanism, we might slip into apathy

- not caring at all. Healthy emotional empathy, on the other hand, encompasses curiosity, listening and expanding our emotional literacy. It practices good boundaries and leans into self-empathy.

Cognitive empathy is putting ourselves in someone else's shoes and trying to hold their perspective. Practicing healthy cognitive empathy involves listening, curiosity, imagination, respect and a growth mindset. If we fail to suspend our own judgements and biases, we might reply with empty advice and phrases such as, "If I were you, I would…" or "You should just…" We might even divert the conversation to start talking about ourselves. In other words, when putting ourselves in someone else's shoes, we need to *remove our own shoes* first. To practice cognitive empathy in a healthy, inclusive way, we acknowledge our own values, privilege and assumptions and listen with an open heart to learn what it's like to be someone else. We seek to understand who they are and where they're coming from. We acknowledge that their reality is different from our own. Embracing and practicing healthy emotional and cognitive empathy then sets us up for the next form of empathy - the response.

Compassionate empathy is the doing. We seek to understand the feelings and perspective of the other person and respond appropriately. Healthy compassionate empathy combines healthy and balanced feeling with understanding while also prioritising our own emotional wellbeing. When we respond in an authentic way, the other person is offered an opportunity to feel heard, valued, visible and safe.

In a nutshell, healthy compassionate empathy, the ability to share and understand the feelings and perspectives of others *and respond appropriately,* is the glue that strengthens our relationships and connects our communities.

But what does healthy compassionate empathy look like? First, we can consider how it feels to receive it. Let's take a deep breath, roll our shoulders and stretch our jaw. Try to remember a time when you felt heard, valued, visible and safe in a conversation with another person. Was

it a friend, a colleague, your partner or maybe even a long-lost teacher? Think about what the other person did during the conversation. What was their demeanour? My guess is that they were simply paying attention. They were probably listening, validating our feelings, asking good questions and not interrupting, offering unsolicited advice, or looking at their phone. They may have calmly asked curious questions and offered emotional validation, perhaps saying:
- "Tell me more?"
- "I'm here for you"
- "Thank you for telling me that"
- "It makes perfect sense you feel that way"

They might even have made a guess about how we felt and even if they got it wrong, we were inclined to trust them a little bit more for trying. As a result, we were more likely to approach them again and felt safe sharing our thoughts and feelings with them. We may have even felt a little less lonely and a bit more connected and understood. Even years later.

And here's the really cool bit - the ability to share and understand the feelings and perspectives of another person and respond appropriately is a *skill we can learn and develop.* It's like a muscle that can be strengthened. And it's a lesson I wish I'd learned much earlier.

So, let's think for a moment about this book - *Women Making a Difference*. In these pages are twenty stories of women who are bravely changing the world. They are battling patriarchy, building leaders and saving lives. Perhaps you're feeling inspired and maybe a little overwhelmed at the same time.

When we think about making a real difference in the world, it can be daunting. We think about large groups of people experiencing pain or injustice: folks experiencing homelessness, children in poverty, women trapped in modern day slavery. We only have to browse the list of targets under the United Nations' Seventeen Sustainable Development Goals to consider the volume of vital work to be done. And sometimes when it feels too big, we get stuck. We get overwhelmed by the complexity of the problems, overcomplicate the solutions and do ... *nothing*.

But here's the thing - to make a profound difference in this world, we can start with just one person. Consider the difference someone made in our lives by making us feel heard, valued, visible and safe.

The key to practicing healthy empathy is to banish the perfectionism and overcomplications that stop us from truly connecting with other people. When we can release the need to say or do the right thing in an attempt to fix a problem, we can just *be*. We can listen to the beautiful human before us, with all of their experiences, trauma, history, attitudes and stories, even if we don't agree with them, so they can feel heard, valued, visible and safe.

Chances are, they're not looking for advice unless they specifically ask for it – but even then, they'll only take our advice if they feel heard first. Our value lies in not how smart we are or if we feel their feelings *for* them, it lies simply in our *presence*, our attention, our interest.
Let's finish with a quick exercise. Let's take a deep breath and listen to *all* of the sounds around us: birds, cars, kids, trains, etc. Take another breath and focus on only the natural sounds for a moment: just the birds, frogs, etc. Take another breath and listen only for the human voices for a few seconds. Excellent. Finally, take a deep breath and listen only for the manmade sounds like planes or leaf-blowers.

How was that? Was it easier to focus on one sound at a time? Did those sounds become clearer?

Listening during our conversations is similar. Humans have a tough time processing too much information simultaneously, so it helps to limit our focus. When we're listening - and calmly deep breathing because it's easier to be empathetic with an oxygenated brain - we can choose whether to listen for the problems to solve and our chance to reply, or for storylines and the emotion that underlies the story.

Listening to the stories of others and acknowledging the emotions in our conversations builds trust and connection. Alisa Yu at Stanford University discovered that by acknowledging others' emotions, especially when dealing with confronting feelings and saying statements like, "You seem upset," or "You look anxious, did something happen?" we tend to foster a higher level of trust in our relationships.

Humans are intensely complex creatures, but healthy empathy doesn't need to be complicated to be impactful. As Brené Brown so eloquently says, "Empathy has no script. There is no right way or wrong way to do it. It's simply listening, holding space, withholding judgment, emotionally connecting, and communicating that incredibly healing message of *you are not alone*."

If we all take a moment to breathe and aim to practice healthy empathy from a place of curiosity, calm, vulnerability and imperfection, we'll realise that life-changing impact can come from making one person feel heard, valued, visible and safe. Take time to embrace healthy empathy with our kids, friends, partners, family, beneficiaries, customers, colleagues and even strangers on the internet, while taking care of, understanding and honouring our own unique, beautiful selves.

That is how we all make a difference.

> "Empathy may be the single most important quality that must be nurtured to give peace a fighting chance."
> **Arundhati Roy**

Leanne Butterworth is an empathy educator, TEDx speaker, university lecturer and social entrepreneur on a mission to create happy, healthy, connected workplaces and communities through interactive, accessible Empathy Training.

A few years ago, Leanne experienced late-diagnosed postnatal mental health issues. Through that, she recognised the life-changing impact of empathy-based listening and communication, versus judgement and stigma.

An active member of the start-up, mental health and social enterprise communities, Leanne is founder of Empathy First, lectures Social Enterprise Business for the Queensland University of Technology and has presented her empathy work in Australia, Canada and the United States.

Leanne is mum to Rowan and Zara, loves beach volleyball, has a degree in Applied Science Exercise Physiology (UQ) and a Postgraduate Certificate in Business (Nonprofit and Philanthropy Studies - QUT). She received a George Alexander Foundation Scholarship, is a member of the Australian Social Impact Fellowship, showcased her work to His Royal Highness, the Duke of York and was awarded the 2023 Women Changing the World People's Choice Social Enterprise Award.

Through her experience and research, Leanne believes empathetic leadership is more than nice-to-have - it's a life imperative.

THE ENERGY OF CONSCIOUSNESS

Lisa Benson

'I've left him.' Nicole's voice seemed softer than normal through my phone. *Maybe she didn't quite believe the words leaving her mouth?*

'You what?'

'I've finally done it. I should have done it years ago.'

'Oh wow. It has been a long time coming. But you couldn't have gone through with it until *you* were really ready,' I said.

'Yeah, I know.' Her words were drawn out. 'It was your book.' She paused for a moment. 'It helped me realise how much I've been putting up with,' she added.

A tingling sensation rose from my belly to my throat. I didn't know how to reply.

I'd always dreamed of writing a book that would be of help to others, but I never imagined my words could carry this kind of power. Most of the women in my writing tribe had 'big' stories – traumatic events they'd experienced which I'd only ever seen in movies: partners leading double lives, devastating bullying, horrific abuse and domestic violence. *Who would ever want to hear my boring and uneventful story?*

I went to school with Nicole, and we've been close throughout our lives. She was never one to seek help and I could count the number of books she's read on my hands.

She had been with Daniel for twenty-five years and they had a child together. She'd been unhappy, reclusive and physically ill for much of this time.

How could my 'little' story be the inciting event that motivated her to finally break free?

Was it just that my book landed in her hands at the right time? Had it been the proverbial 'final straw'? Did my words name something she hadn't been able to in her own life? It didn't matter to me – all I knew is that my book had made a difference.

When we think of 'making a difference' we often imagine huge success, fame or a worldwide impact like a new technology for desalination or removing plastic from the oceans. Few of us will ever achieve these – but that doesn't mean we won't make a difference.

I believe each of us has valuable offerings to bring into the light. When I think about those who've made a difference in my life, they're ordinary people who haven't done anything dramatic. They are the ones who have stuck by me and supported me through my most difficult times. I can be vulnerable with them; they make me feel safe and encourage me when I get off track.

Most of us are more deeply affected by how others make us feel than by anything material or tangible. The energy we give off and receive is a vastly underrated power tool in our personal arsenal.

A person's energy is difficult to describe because it's invisible, but we can sense it. As an empath, I strongly feel 'vibes'. When I'm in the presence of negative energy, I've been known to shudder so violently that I need two hands to lift a glass of water without spilling it. By contrast, I am viscerally calmed when I encounter positive energy.

Energy is subtle, so we don't always appreciate it. We think the magic lies in big life events, so we disproportionately celebrate career accolades and goals reached, while often bypassing the mini milestones along the way. We revere the number of years married over the quality and happiness of the ordinary days required to reach each anniversary. In reality, most of our life is spent 'on the way' to a goal or destination.

So, how can the average person possibly 'make a difference' in other people's lives? Perhaps it's not something we can plan. I know I make a difference by how I show up in the world for myself and others. It is not a mathematical equation or a transaction with a guaranteed outcome.

Because we can't see energy, we never receive a ranking based on how much we have initiated change. There is no KPI (key performance indicator) for who does it the best.

As human beings, we are all interconnected and form part of the great web of life. We play a unique role and are positioned in the precise place and time to fit into the universal puzzle. A dance teacher may help hundreds of people learn to dance over decades, and thus, make an impression on many lives. But taking the time to hold space and simply listen to someone who is struggling may be all that is needed to change the trajectory of that person's life.

Given that we do not know the impact of our acts, maybe we should behave as if all our words and deeds could make a difference.

In primary school, I used to cup my left hand around my exam papers in a makeshift shield to guard my answers from whoever was sitting next to me. I strangled my pen as I rapidly moved my right hand over the page – my heart beating heavy in my chest. *Faster, faster,* I kept encouraging myself. Mrs Glasson's voice would then slice through the silence.

'Okay everyone, finish up. Two minutes to go.'

Even though my eyes were focused on the page, I trusted my peripheral vision to identify any heads that turned in my direction with eyes that could steal my precious answers.

I have come a long way since that primary school classroom. Instead of cupping my hands, I open them. I have learned to trust the abundance of the world, where there is enough for all of us. Passing on the knowledge we acquire is a selfless act. The joy is in sharing what we know and have, not in the hoarding. In the words of nineteenth century poet Rabindranath Tagore, 'All that is not given is lost.'

But it has taken over four decades for me to break down the barriers that a life of perfectionism built around me. For too long, I had a scarcity mentality and was way too concerned about how other people viewed me.

LISA BENSON

What I learned is that we can't be authentic or have significant impact on others when our focus is on external validation rather than nurturing our essence. I believed I had to be perfect to impress others, but I've discovered this couldn't be further from the truth. As a perfectionist, I was disconnected from myself and others, and could never reach my potential until I learned how powerful it was to be vulnerable. I deeply connected with others through my mistakes and shames, more than anything I'd done right. In my memoir, I open up about my own struggles, which has prompted others to disclose personal stories they've never felt safe to share. We connect through our imperfections and humanness.

My motto has become *Stop Trying – Start Being* because as a perfectionist, I spent most of my life doing the opposite. I tried to gain acceptance when all I really ever needed was to accept myself … and be myself. To me, making a difference is no different. I have stopped thinking I am not doing enough just because I can't physically see the impact I've had on others. We may never see the results of our efforts, but we can learn to trust that what we are putting out into the world will be of benefit if and when it is meant to.

There is an Indian proverb, 'Blessed are those who plant trees under whose shade they will never sit.' The biggest impact we make may be posthumous. I know that my memoir, *Where Have I Been All My Life?*, has made a difference. Hundreds of readers have reached out to let me know how their lives have changed since reading my book. Some have said 'I felt like I was reading my own story' or 'your vulnerability and bravery helped me understand my own life'. While I always hoped to give people new ways of seeing and thinking, I never imagined my readers would actually leave long-term relationships as a result of my words. In another heartfelt email, one reader wrote, 'You saved my life.'

Who knows what impact my story may have in the future? It's not my task to control its trajectory. I have done my part in this lifetime and the ripple effect will unfold in time.

WOMEN MAKING A DIFFERENCE

I had no idea this was going to happen while I was writing. In fact, I was plagued with self-doubt throughout the process.

Now I see that we underestimate the goodness we can bring to the world because we don't see the value of our contribution, while all the time, it's whirring within the universal energy and generating an energetic force. It grows and gains momentum once it is sent off into the world, making an invisible difference.

The greatest offering we can gift others is to keep working on ourselves. But what does that actually involve? To me, it means taking responsibility for my life instead of blaming others and making meaning out of the experiences I have encountered. Doing 'the work' is a lifelong challenge. We can study, read or journal, as long as we are continually making tiny changes that add up to huge ones. Being conscious doesn't mean we get it right every time, it's having a greater awareness while continually learning and transforming.

It can be difficult to have an influence on other people's lives if we haven't been on a journey of consciousness ourselves. As Joseph Campbell's *Hero's Journey* outlines, we need to have suffered, overcome and become resilient, so we can be a role model to others. We must emerge as a changed person on the other side. Through our pain and frustration, we become a lived example to inspire others. We can't simply get advice and meet our future selves on the other side while high-jumping or spiritually bypassing over the terrible stuff. We must wade through the mud.

When we show our vulnerability through our stories, we connect with others more powerfully than if we simply tell them what we think is best for them. Showing how we've negotiated our way through adversity is a gentle, inclusive way to pass on the messages we have gleaned from our lives. In this way we can transfer the energy of our experiences without being didactic. This allows the other person to travel at their own pace and feel empowered that they are making their own choices. What we put out into the world is merely an invitation, and the reader will absorb the messages if they resonate. We all know that one light-bulb moment at the right time can alter a life. Each of us is motivated by different triggers, depending on our current circumstances.

As in Nicole's case, timing was everything. I was an ear to listen to over many years, but I never once told her to leave. She was the only one that knew what she was experiencing, and the only one who could make that decision. My story landed in her hands precisely when she needed it. I didn't plan that. I just did my part and wrote a book. When we share stories from inside our pain, we help others recognise their own struggles and give them permission to initiate change and take risks.

Despite my fears, it turns out my ordinary 'little' story is resonating with many. We don't have to have a big story for it to be impactful. We just have to be brave enough to begin and vulnerable enough to share. I often thought of giving up when I compared myself to other writers with 'bigger' stories, but something inside me pushed me to keep going. I knew that if nothing else came from my book, the personal growth I would gain from writing it would already be worth it. The impact it's had on others has simply been a wonderful bonus.

Compound interest doesn't only apply to money, but to contribution too. In the movie, *Pay It Forward,* Haley Joel Osment plays a child who took on a project where he performed a kind act for three people. In turn, the recipients had to pass the kindness on to three more and so on. I don't want to reveal the spoiler if you haven't watched the movie, but the ending is about the ripple effect of small actions. In the same way, I have begun to appreciate that when I connect with one person, not only does this make a huge difference to them, but it inspires them to pass the high vibrational energy on to others.

Sometimes, a task in front of us may seem impossible; like when we want to declutter the entire house rather than one room at a time. We can get overwhelmed if we think too big. But in the same way that changing small habits, such as drinking more water or waking up earlier to exercise or meditate, aids our health, doing tiny acts of kindness, like gifting a stranger's coffee or looking someone in the eye with genuine love, may be the beginning of a roll-on effect. Little things have a way of multiplying into big things when we are conscious of the energy we are contributing to the world. We may never see the result, but do we really need to? When we release the egoic need for significance, we don't need accolades or proof of our impact.

It's not my task to manipulate a particular outcome or ever see the results of my actions. My role is to show up as the most authentic version of me. If I am conscious of this, I will reach those to whose lives I'm meant to make a difference. Sometimes trying to achieve 'big' things defeats the purpose. The things that have the most impact are the 'little' things that you may never have thought would make a difference. These provide lasting legacies and impact other souls.

Our voice does not have to be loud to be heard. Mighty forces can emerge from soft places. Simply by living in our authentic power, we are making a difference because it gives others permission to do the same. If only we knew the power we each possess. When we are consciously working towards healing ourselves, we raise the vibration we are emitting into the world, and it affects all those we connect with. This boundless energy is then available for understanding, resonance and making others feel more human and less alone. The far-reaching impact of small actions can be astounding.

I've come to understand I can make a difference, even without any action on my part. We impact each other by who we are, not what we do. When we show up in the world in a way that honours every single human as a worthy equal and we put the work in to make meaning of our own life, we can't help but influence others in a positive way. The energy we emulate by simply being conscious may have more impact than we could ever imagine.

Nicole and I are both approaching fifty and are descendants of a generation of people-pleasers, where women didn't speak up or stand up for themselves. I have a feeling she was a survivor of coercive control just like me. Maybe I was the disrupter – the circuit breaker – and saved her from a violent ending to her relationship. I'll never know.

With my friend on the line, I finally found my voice and I said to Nicole, 'I know how much strength this must have taken.'

And if nothing else ever comes from my book, in that moment, everything made a perfect and mysterious sense. I know I've made a difference.

Lisa Benson is a self-diagnosed recovering perfectionist who spent five years writing her multi-award-winning memoir, *Where Have I Been All My Life?* During this time, she lived part-time on a boat in Sydney Harbour which she found to be a peaceful and inspirational space for her writing. Lisa and her husband continue to lead a 'double life' travelling between Newcastle and Sydney each week.

Lisa has a bachelor of business degree with a major in tourism and marketing. She previously held various sales and marketing positions in hotels and resorts, and also worked in a real estate office. It wasn't until Lisa was in her forties that she decided to pursue her lifelong dream of becoming an author, and she now writes full-time.

Lisa's motto is *Stop Trying – Start Being* although she spent most of her life doing the exact opposite. Her writing is honest and relatable, and she hopes her vulnerability helps others feel less alone. Lisa would love to inspire women to stop wasting time living up to other people's expectations, to discover the magic of living an authentic life and to be free of self-imposed limitations.

If you would like to hear more from Lisa, you can follow her on Instagram (lisabensonauthor), Facebook (Lisa Benson Author) or LinkedIn (Lisa Benson).

Lisa's website is lisabensonauthor.com

A LOVE LETTER TO WOMEN IN BUSINESS

Melanie Wentzel

A career in business can be impossibly hard work. It requires consistency, tenacity, drive and a very thick skin. When I chose a career in business, I quickly learnt that not every woman will be your ally, some will try to keep you from rising and even tear you down on their own climb to the top.

Equally, there are women in business who will cherish you, support you, teach you, inspire and be inspired by you; those who will recognise your value and your voice, and create opportunities for you – and I am one of them. This is my love letter to you.

I was recently asked by a photographer how I wanted to be perceived. Without thinking, I replied, 'I want men to perceive me as powerful and women to perceive me as collaborative.' I didn't know that about myself until I was asked, and it has taken me on a journey of reflection over my decade of experience in business.

I have had some exceptional male peers and colleagues at all stages of their careers (and mine) who have championed me, guided me, worked incredibly hard for me, and offered me opportunities simply because they knew I was the best person for the job.

I have also (here it comes …) had male colleagues who have ignored me, spoken over me, pointed out a typo in my slides during a presentation to national healthcare leaders and even physically advanced upon me in a threatening manner until I was bailed up against an office door having to call out STOP three times before he did. This occurred in front of others in a corporate office. He received a verbal warning and he kept his job. This was explained away by HR and by my Manager – no support was offered, no apology made – I simply had to work alongside him for years after – always feeling unsafe. I think my *now conscious* want to be perceived by men as powerful is because I believe that in business, power and influence is their currency. It's what they value in themselves and what they perceive as valuable in others. By branding myself to men as powerful, I become their equal in business. I am perceived not as 'less' (powerful), but as a colleague and peer. That branding levels the 'perception playing field'.

Wanting women to perceive me as collaborative, came as no real surprise. I love women and I love working with women. Alongside and inspired by the leadership of some incredible women over the past decade, I have built a career of value and joy.

I approach the work I do with women with the belief that we are in it together, all on the rise. I want everyone to win. I admire women who came before me and those who have generously mentored me, and I equally admire those just starting their business journey. I take exceptional joy in my female working relationships. Above my desk, I display a collection of polaroids taken at various offices, at home and events, of the women I love to do business with – they are 'my people'.

My background in is psychology and project management. I have dedicated my career to high-performing healthcare, which is person-centred and meaningful to patients, their families and communities. I have co-designed, implemented and led over nine million dollars' worth of healthcare transformation projects across mainstream healthcare and the cannabis sector; including the design and rollout of a veterans' food bank, and the co-design and implementation of specialist medical cannabis clinics in Australia, the United States and United Kingdom. I was privileged to lead a national Aboriginal and Torres Strait Islander health project which saw hospital and hospice staff trained to accommodate spiritual and cultural practices in palliative and end-of-life care settings. I've trained medical colleges to coach doctors to improve interpersonal communication with their patients. I've studied health technologies with

Harvard Medical School, and co-designed and led the creation of patient experience surveys and technologies, and digital patient pathways for the cannabis industry. I have been published in the *Medical Journal of Australia* and spoken at conferences, education days, on webinars and podcasts. The work I do matters, because there is nothing more personal than our health and the care, we, and our loved ones, receive. That is my 'why'.

In this love letter, I will share the two things I believe matter most as a woman in business: Building your personal brand and building your professional community.

Taking control of your personal brand and influencing the story people believe about you is incredibly powerful. People will form an opinion of you regardless, and unless you take control of the narrative, it will be based on a tiny amount of information they have about you, interpreted through the lens of their own beliefs, history and experiences of people 'like' you, or rather, like the person they perceive you to be. Sometimes it will be favourable and at other times not – but it will *never* be the full story. And whatever they choose to believe impacts you and your career.

I'm a great example of someone who spent years *not* thinking about my personal brand, and to be very honest, it was career limiting. I'm great at what I do, but for a long time, people only caught the (perceived) highlights. What they didn't know about me was my passion for learning and leading. They didn't know that I have lived and worked, not only in Australia but in the United States, United Kingdom, France and South Africa, and that I put myself through university in my thirties, achieving a high distinction average and making the dean's list, while a single parent to a five-year-old and working two jobs. They interpreted my confidence as arrogance because they didn't know what I already knew about myself – that I can do anything, and that I'm on a mission to do great work and build a career which is rewarding (professionally, financially, spiritually, socially) and where the work I do changes lives for the better. I finally realised that it was *my* job to tell them, and so my personal brand emerged.

Your personal brand is not (necessarily) about creating a logo or a LinkedIn following, it's about knowing who you are, staying true to her, telling others who she is and then <u>turning up as her every day</u>. It's for you to know and then communicate in word and in action:

- Your 'why' – the contribution you want to make to the world both personally and professionally. If you're not sure yet, that's okay – do some reading and meditate on it – you'll find it.
- Your values – easily the most important element of personal branding and your north star as you navigate the business world.
- Your ways of working – how you operate in the business world (and what people can expect of you).
- Your special skills – I'm a systems thinker, a leader who identifies and grows potential in others, and I love to celebrate achievement by telling the stories of the work I am a part of.

Your values are what make you unique – they are your special mix of drivers that will keep you steady when things get rough (and they will). My values are the personal and constant truths I believe about myself and my work. They are the measure which I check against if I have a difficult decision to make or am reflecting on my work or actions. They have never once let me down. They are:

Integrity: Doing the right thing even when no-one is looking (including in the quality of your work). When you act with integrity you never have to look back over your shoulder wondering what might catch up with you. You become professionally bulletproof because you did the right thing, at the right time and you did it well.

Authenticity: Turning up as a whole person and the same version of yourself every single time matters. You can only do that if you are truly yourself – anything else is just not sustainable. It's about honesty and having the courage to work within your personal values and boundaries, and to ask questions and ask for help when you need it. Authenticity engenders trust and builds quality relationships. Importantly, it creates a safe space for *others* to be their authentic selves.

Generosity – without score keeping: This has, by far, been the greatest asset to me in my career to date. Even if you don't feel it will benefit you right now, sharing your knowledge and your story, being generous with your expertise and supporting others through review, feedback, providing resources or invitations to collaborate, means you will receive the same back, and it will likely be when you need it most. Recommend people in your network for promotions, jobs or board positions. With clients, do more than the bare minimum and make yourself available, even when the job is done. This will help to build relationships. It's not about someone owing you a favour, when you give selflessly, others see it and remember it. When they have something to offer you, they do so, not because of some perceived debt, but because they value you. It's a virtuous cycle of generosity and it builds careers.

Quality: Like excellence, quality is a choice. The quality of your work is completely within your control. Multiple iterations of review and feedback don't make you popular with those who don't understand quality and collaboration, but if quality matters to you, as it does to me, persist. By choosing quality and excellence, you:

- Ensure your work aligns with (and builds) your personal brand.
- Grow the people around you.
- Establish a set of standards that others can expect from you.

- Set an example for others who may be looking to you, especially for leadership.

Your ways of working are more operational than your values. They are the practical elements of your professionalism and how you operate in a professional environment. They are unique to you and will adapt and mature over time. Like your values, they are a great tool for business decision-making and reflection. Mine are:

Know the numbers: Money is not a dirty word and understanding finance matters. In business, money is simply a measure exchanged for time, goods or outcomes, so you need to understand it to operate effectively in your own or in someone else's business. Never shy away from a financial conversation – always be clear and specific, ask questions, and be open to negotiation to ensure the dollar and outcome value works for everyone.

Structure your work: Plan your work, create frameworks and structure, pre-fill calendars and invoice dates and write schedules which you share to all stakeholders to keep you (and others) accountable. At one time I was running twenty-five concurrent healthcare transformation projects for the Department of Health, state governments and other organisations, with a team of three project managers and another nine creative and support staff, plus academic and clinical subject matter experts. As a team, we never delivered a project late or below expectation because I ran a structured team of high-performing professionals who were empowered and activated. Because the work was structured, they knew what I expected, knew what they could expect from me, and we turned up for each other and our clients.

When you are a leader, the buck stops with YOU: It's your job to design the work, your job to fully scope out the work, including future needs and risk, your job to recruit or train the right team, your job to manage the team, your job to sign off on the work, your job to understand and manage the budget, your job to check and sign off every deliverable and your job to create a culture where your team are free to fail – which means they are free to create and push to the very edge of boundaries, to innovate and experiment. And if *any* part of the work fails – then it's on you, and true leaders never shy away from accountability. That's the burden and the privilege of leadership.

Whatever your values, whatever your brand, your professional community matters. My professional community is made up of some truly incredible women – I mean, some of these women are a *big deal*, and I am grateful every day for the opportunity to have them in my life as peers, colleagues, friends and family. My community has a little of each.

Professional relationships and communities grow and evolve in the most beautiful and unexpected ways. Two of my most treasured friendships were born in my professional community. One was my best customer in the very early days of a streetwear label I founded while at university; and one was a cannabis consulting client, and co-founder of the first company to ever import cannabis legally to Australia from Thailand. As your profesional community grows, keep your eyes open for the 'blossoms at the edge of the garden' because women are great at surprising you with support and kindness and joy.

Let me tell you about 'The Barbies'. We are six former colleagues who meet up once a month and turn up for each other in our (hilarious) group chat as needed. One works in cannabis, one works for the Olympics, one owns a tattoo studio, three are now spread across healthcare. Three have worked on my project and operations teams, three are parents, one is raising a beautiful young trans-man and one is about to be married; and while our lives are different in so many ways, we are a small and kind community – of women – supporting each other's professional journeys.

MELANIE WENTZEL

I am also blessed to be a part of the most incredible global women's group chat - the EmpowHer Cannabis Society (ECS) with 600 of us all on the same professional journey. It's a 24/7 rolling collaborative space where we ask questions, share advice, share opportunities, and celebrate success to build up each other, and our careers.

Honestly, connections and communities like these are magic, and clearly, I am a woman who thrives in community.

I asked three women from my professional community to describe my personal brand. Here's what they said:

- Magnetic, empowering, leader.
- Ethical, professional, innovative.
- Self-motivated, passionate, collaborative.

Nailed it.

And now I extend an invitation to connect with me, to join my professional community of women on the rise. You are very welcome here.

Love, Mel x

MELANIE WENTZEL

Melanie Wentzel: Leader, learner and healthcare transformation specialist.

Melanie is an enthusiastic professional driven by a vision of high quality, equitable healthcare. She believes in people and their communities, and has dedicated her career to promoting person-centred, respectful and culturally responsive care.

Melanie is a global thinker and passionate storyteller, seeking the knowledge of those who came before her and applying it through evidence-based frameworks to drive quality improvement and the delivery of innovative and emerging models of care.

Melanie is a contemporary and collaborative consultant, taking a boutique approach to healthcare transformation in the public health and medical cannabis sectors, servicing both Australian and international markets. She has worked extensively with the Australian Department of Health, state governments, medical colleges, primary health networks, peak bodies and organisations across the Australian, American and British healthcare landscapes delivering impactful and transformative programs for patients, communities, clinicians and the global healthcare system.

Melanie is a bachelor of psychological science, an experienced project manager, a national healthcare operations leader, a member of the Australasian Society of Lifestyle Medicine and graduate of the Harvard Medical School Digital Transformation in Healthcare Program.

Melanie has twice published in the *Medical Journal of Australia* (MJA), is an experienced conference speaker, panellist and podcast guest.

MELANIE WENTZEL

melaniewentzel.com
linkedin.com/in/melaniewentzel

LIFE
Nicola Baker

L ife.
It's an incredible journey and adventure of experiences. The highs and lows, the colours of light and dark. Everyone's journey through life is different. Some are blessed to be in a blue lagoon with crystal-clear water, calm blue skies and a gentle breeze, sailing on luxury yachts, drinking champagne and kissed by the warm embrace of the sun.

For others, the journey is fraught with danger and difficulty, with crashing waves, dark, ominous clouds and wind that cuts you to the bone. We hold on to a rickety old ship as it rises in the stormy seas. We are cold, we can't see the horizon and we are lost.

Or are we? Sometimes, life can be a facade, an image that is presented to the world. The difference, however, between living in a facade or reality can quite often be one simple thing – attitude.

A positive attitude doesn't always come naturally. Attitudes are often directed by life experience and can put us on a particular trajectory. For example, my attitude was vastly different in my younger years. I was a corporate achiever; my attitude was primarily self-centred and I didn't understand the ripple effect my work had on others, nor did I really care. I worked on the top floor of a corporate building, was a high achiever and was recognised, not only by my employers, but also by the wider community. I thought I was happy and felt fulfilled. What I've come to realise, however, is that I didn't understand the true meaning of happiness. My luxury yacht had a private chef, there was a different exotic port for us to enjoy every day, and life seemed perfect.

I met my husband, Peter, on 1 May 1999 in a dark, dingy nightclub. He rather quickly revealed that it wasn't easy having dependants, and I was immediately put off; I didn't want to meet anyone else's children. I was a single woman doing what I wanted to do when I wanted, and 'second-hand' kids were not my idea of a good time. But then, he said, 'I have six budgies.' It was love at second sight, and it progressed very quickly from there. He introduced his budgies to me, became a family and eventually proposed. I was on top of the world, sailing along on my luxury yacht with Peter sitting on the top deck beside me.

Within a year, we were married, and our lives changed forever when we welcomed our firstborn into the world.

Jed struggled through the first six weeks, but as new parents, Peter and I looked forward to a normal sleep pattern returning. The calm waters of our journey started to become murky, and the ship became gnarled and weathered by the choppy seas. We desperately held on, but it was getting rough.

That first six weeks with Jed seemed to drag, but before we knew it, the following months passed with no improvement. It just went on, and on, and on.

The night-time became the devil, the sharks circled our ship, and the onset of darkness brought dread and fear. Sleep deprivation became a form of torture for us. It played havoc on our judgement and relationships, causing unintentional damage.

Many friends and family offered advice, forward in making our failures known. All the while, Jed was battling in his own way; an undiagnosed disease was causing him pain, making it simply impossible to achieve the rest that he – and we – desperately needed.

Then, at just eleven months old, Jed suffered a stroke.

We quickly learnt that stroke is not just an 'old person's' disease and can happen in kids too. Jed's stroke was catastrophic, causing him significant brain damage and leaving him paralysed down one side of his body. This cruel episode meant that Jed would never meet his milestones as other children of the same age would.

At the time, Peter and I didn't realise just how much Jed's stroke and consequent health challenges would change our lives. We didn't know what caused the stroke, we still weren't sleeping, and for the three of us, life was a very rough ocean in a storm. There was no lifeboat, and no safe harbour. We went on like this … for years.

Sadly, the reality was that no-one could understand what we were going through, except Peter and me. Outwardly, we were doing well. Yes, we had some trouble with Jed, and yes, we had challenges, but so did many young families. Outwardly, the sun was shining, and we were smooth sailing.

We decided that in order to live our best lives, we would benefit from being in a small community, so we moved to the country, set up a small business, and Peter landed the job he wanted. Jed was growing, and although we did see his deficits, to the outside world, everything was just dandy.

I became so comfortable in our new surroundings that I was able to sit in a group of women and make commentary on others, passing judgement. I was able to see a heated discussion on social media and felt happy to jump in, boots and all. I enjoyed the drama of it all, channelling my attention to others' problems and shortcomings, rather than focusing on my own.

Although, I knew better than to assume that those who look good on the outside are also looking good on the inside. I was beginning to admit to myself that I was wearing a mask for the outside world. The dark sunglasses would come down after a rough morning with Jed. I would limit my exposure to others, excluding myself from our community. I would try my best to keep it together on the outside, but on the inside, I was dying a silent and solitary death.

Jed was finally diagnosed with moyamoya disease just after his third birthday. We sat on his diagnosis for a year, just managing to get through each day. Jed wasn't provided with help to ease his symptoms during that time, and I felt *angry* at our new fate. How could this happen to us? What did we do to deserve this child who we couldn't help? They were the questions I kept asking myself. Peter and I were the golden couple; how on earth did we become a family raising a child with special needs? By now, enormous waves were crashing over our ship, and we were sinking.

Jed was a complicated little boy who needed our help to live with moyamoya disease. We were sent to Sydney Children's Hospital, and there we discovered that moyamoya was progressive, often leaving the sufferer feeling incredibly lonely and isolated due to its rarity. We went through years of travelling to Sydney, where Jed underwent a renal artery bypass and three brain surgeries, sadly suffering another stroke. Constant blood tests left Jed with an incredible trauma response. Working through this experience with him, and his team, left both Peter and me floundering, feeling alone. We felt like we were in a glass box looking out, while the rest of the world just got on with 'normal' life.

I made it very clear to Peter that if Jed didn't make it, neither would I. I had no intention of letting Jed go on a journey to another place without his mummy to hold him. I can admit now that I saw calmer waters on the other side, and wherever Jed was, it was where I wanted to be.

Peter and I thought early on that Jed would be our only child. We were thrilled then, to welcome a second and third child to our family, both healthy babies, Charlie and Lucy. Had the storm begun to pass?

On 9 June 2015, I was working from my little cottage when I heard a loud boom. A car had crashed into the local I and the explosion was devastating. Our town lost good people that day, including my friend, a lady who had been such a positive influence in my life, and now, even more so in death.

I allowed myself to wallow in the cesspit of grief and trauma for as long as I needed to, but then the moment for me to pivot came. I realised my friend did not get to fulfil her dreams. Her life had been taken from her in an instant, and those she left behind had a choice to make.

In 2019, I realised I had been grieving for long enough, for the loss of what I thought my child was going to be, and also for the loss of my friend. And whilst grief is a very different vessel for every person, I recognised that, now, it was my time to get up, dust myself off and get back on track.

I decided that as I had been through an experience with a rare disease like moyamoya, I was perfectly placed to help others going through that early diagnosis and treatment. I could offer a kind word here and there, and I could let others understand what certain phrases, tests and expectations could be. With my experience, I founded Moyamoya Australia in September 2019 and haven't looked back.

Today, I am the master of my ship. Although it's not a luxury yacht, more a speedboat, Peter is at the wheel, I'm enjoying the scenery, and the kids are on a biscuit at the back of the boat, laughing as they ride in our wake. We can change direction at a moment's notice, throwing out lifelines to those who need us.

I still wear my mask some days. Life has delivered more blows and losses but now I use my mask as a way of coping, not hiding from the more difficult days. I have come to terms with the idea that life is not guaranteed, tomorrow may never come, and I will strive to leave the best mark on this world as I possibly can. My children are watching and learning from me, so I choose to use my speedboat to find a way to joy, happiness and kindness. Knowing I could be the life raft for another family is where I have found my purpose. I have realised that I am alive to have these experiences, and they can help others on this moyamoya ship. Sometimes, I can take my little family on the luxury yacht and be thankful for all the blessings we have.

Nicola Baker is a published author in Far North Queensland, Australia. Her first book, *The Thing About Jed*, was launched in May 2022 published by Bowerbird Publishers. She was inspired to establish Moyamoya Australia to assist others with the rare disease of Moyamoya in their journey by providing financial assistance, raising awareness, funding research and training into this disease. Nicola is working on a collaboration regarding childhood stroke with Bowerbird Publishing, she is a participating member of the Childhood Stroke Advisory Panel for the Lived Experience of Childhood Stroke. Nicola has won multiple awards for her charity work, and is using her experience to help others. Nicola is excited to be working with twenty powerful women in the publication of *Women Making a Difference*.

BEYOND BAOBABS

GIRLS WHO DARE TO DREAM

Patricia Gonde

IGNITING THE FLAME OF LEADERSHIP

In Harare's vibrant heart, Goodhope Primary School stood tall, a beacon of scholarly excellence, its silhouette echoing the ancient baobabs that dotted the African landscape. At its helm, Ms Taranja, a woman with a vision as unwavering as the baobab's roots, ignited a revolution of empowerment. These majestic trees, known for their longevity and resilience, symbolized for Ms Taranja the potential within each girl – a potential that transcended societal limitations Her dream was not merely to educate but to nurture the leaders of tomorrow, particularly the young women who, she believed, were the keystones of a brighter, more equitable future.

Under Ms Taranja's guidance, the school's philosophy became transformative, championing the holistic development of its students. Goodhope became a crucible of growth, where education transcended traditional boundaries, fostering physical, cultural and intellectual excellence. Ms Taranja fervently advocated for leadership through empowerment, a lesson she instilled in the hearts and minds of her students.

The leadership legacy program was the embodiment of this ethos. Aspiring young women were encouraged to lead, debate and innovate, becoming adept in critical thinking and problem-solving. The debate team, once underestimated, evolved into a formidable group, their arguments as piercing as acacia thorns, their confidence unyielding.

Ms Taranja's vision expanded beyond the school walls, venturing into the global arena. She curated opportunities for her girls to travel, learn and engage internationally. From the bustling streets of Delhi to the historic charm of Portugal, these journeys widened perspectives, reshaping their worldviews, culminating in a triumphant presentation at an environmental expo in Dubai. The global odyssey of the Goodhope girls, traversing to these places, served as a testament to the school's commitment to global citizenship. Their presentations, particularly on Africa's sustainable practices, showcased their depth of understanding and passion, earning them international acclaim.

MENTORSHIP AND PEER LEARNING

Upon returning, the experiences of these young ambassadors became beacons for their peers, transforming Goodhope into an incubator of inspiration. They shared their stories, disseminating the wisdom they had gained, fostering a culture where every girl believed in her potential to effect change locally and globally. Ms Taranja's efforts bore fruit as her girls became confident agents of change, embodying the leadership legacy program's core belief that their voices were pivotal in shaping the future. Goodhope's evolving reputation attracted attention far and wide, with Ms Taranja ever willing to share her innovative educational model.

A LEGACY ROOTED IN COMMUNITY

Beyond Goodhope's gates, Ms Taranja's influence was profound. She recognised the importance of accessible education and addressed this by instituting a scholarship program for underprivileged girls. These scholarships were not just gateways to education but conduits for unlocking latent potential and ambition.

One such beneficiary was Nyasha, a bright and inquisitive girl from a struggling family. Nyasha's dreams of becoming a doctor seemed impossible amidst her circumstances. However, the Goodhope scholarship opened doors she never thought possible. The school's nurturing environment and Ms Taranja's unwavering support allowed Nyasha to excel in her studies, her once-flickering flame of hope now burning brightly. Her story became a beacon of hope for countless other girls in similar situations. The scholarship program, funded through Ms Taranja's tireless fundraising efforts, and the generous support of Goodhope alumni and friends across the globe, continued to transform lives, one bright mind at a time. There is another story – from grit to grace.

COMMUNITY ENGAGEMENT

The impact of Ms Taranja's vision extended to local initiatives, such as support for a children's home and fostering a culture of social responsibility among her students. These efforts instilled in them a deep empathy and a commitment to serving their community. Every Friday afternoon, a group of Goodhope girls, led by Ms Taranja herself, visited the Tariro Children's Home in the nearby township. They spent time with the children, playing games, reading stories and offering a much-needed dose of love and laughter. Though seemingly small, these visits were instrumental in bridging the gap between privilege and disadvantage, instilling in the Goodhope girls a sense of humility and social responsibility.

EMPOWERING FAMILIES

The initiatives led by Ms Taranja also targeted mothers and families within the community. Recognising that a girl's education could only reach its full potential with a supportive foundation at home, Ms Taranja designed programs that empowered mothers and strengthened family structures.

One such program was the Mothers' Literacy Circle. Every Tuesday morning, under the shade of a sprawling mango tree in the schoolyard, a group of mothers gathered for literacy classes. Ms Taranja and a team of dedicated volunteers provided basic reading and writing skills, financial literacy training and workshops on health and child care. The aim was not just to empower mothers with knowledge but also to create a safe space for them to build a supportive network, share experiences and find solutions to their everyday challenges. The impact of this program was profound. As mothers gained confidence in their literacy and learned valuable skills, they became more involved in their children's education, attending parent-teacher meetings and actively participating in school events. They felt empowered to advocate for their children and navigate the sometimes-intimidating world of bureaucracy.

But Ms Taranja's vision extended beyond literacy. Recognising the economic hardships faced by many families, she spearheaded the Beyond Horizons Micro-Enterprise Initiative. This program provided small loans and business training to mothers with entrepreneurial aspirations. With guidance on budgeting, marketing and basic bookkeeping, women started making and selling crafts, baked goods and local produce. These micro-enterprises, though modest, meant the world to their families, providing a much-needed source of income and a sense of agency for the women themselves.

The stories of the mothers involved in these programs were testaments to their transformative power. Amai Tendekai became a vocal advocate for girls' education after overcoming her initial shyness in the literacy circle, speaking at community gatherings and inspiring other mothers to send their daughters to school. Mbuya vaShona used her micro-loan to set up a small vegetable stall, earning enough to send her two children to high school and finally escape the cycle of poverty.

The success of these initiatives resonated throughout the community, fostering a sense of collective progress and hope. Mothers' voices, once unheard, now played a vital role in shaping the future of their families. This ripple effect of empowerment, starting with Ms Taranja's belief in the potential of young girls, extended outwards, strengthening the very fabric of the community.

OVERCOMING ADVERSITY AND BUILDING RESILIENCE

Ms Taranja's personal journey was one of resilience and determination.

Growing up in a rural village, she defied societal expectations that confined women to traditional roles. Despite having only one pair of well-worn sandals, she walked kilometres to school daily – her thirst for knowledge unquenchable. Her father, a small farmer who scraped by to fund her education, initially envisioned her as a nurse, but it was the passion for teaching that truly resonated with her, leading her to switch career paths courageously.

Her triumphs against economic and cultural barriers became a powerful narrative for everyone. Trish Taranja's journey from trials to triumph showed how perseverance and education could defy the odds. Her story was inspirational and a road map for her students, showing them that their circumstances did not define their future. She rose above family and societal expectations. Despite familial pressure, her choice to pursue a career in education highlighted the importance of following one's passion. Her decision to leave nursing and embrace teaching was a bold move that demonstrated to her students the value of authenticity and the pursuit of one's true calling. This message resonated deeply with the young women of Goodhope, encouraging them to chart their paths and stand firm against societal and familial pressures.

THE UNFOLDING OF DREAMS

Within Goodhope Primary School, the culture of achievement hummed like a potent energy. Each student's success fuelled the collective ambition, fostering an environment where learning wasn't merely an obligation but a passport to a brighter future. Ms Taranja's mentorship was pivotal, her own story a compass guiding the girls towards unimaginable heights.

One such example was Tapiwa, a young woman whose brilliance in Science shone like a star. Ms Taranja recognised her talent and encouraged her to participate in regional science competitions. Tapiwa's innovative project on sustainable solar energy won her accolades and a scholarship to a prestigious science academy, paving the way for a future at the forefront of environmental solutions. Tapiwa's story was one of many. Goodhope became a fertile ground for future leaders, doctors, engineers and artists. The school walls resonated with the quiet thrum of determination, each student driven by the shared belief that their dreams were not fleeting fantasies but blueprints for a more equitable world. Ms Taranja instilled in them the philosophy of 'daring to dream big', nurturing their ambitions beyond the limitations of their immediate circumstances.

This culture of achievement extended beyond academic pursuits. Goodhope's sports field witnessed the blossoming of future Olympians, their athletic prowess echoing across the dusty ground. Once relegated to forgotten corners, the school choir transformed into a powerful force, their voices soaring through Harare's streets, carrying messages of hope and social justice. They even competed internationally and won gold medals.

ENCOURAGING GLOBAL CITIZENSHIP

Ms Taranja understood that education needed to equip students for their local communities and the interconnected world they would inherit. The travel experiences she curated were not mere excursions but windows into global realities, challenging perspectives and broadening horizons.

The trip to India exposed the girls to ancient wisdom and contemporary struggles, teaching them about sustainable practices and resilience in the face of poverty. Portugal served as a bridge to their colonial past, prompting critical dialogue about identity and the legacies of history. Dubai, with its futuristic skyline and ambitious environmental initiatives, ignited their passion for innovation and social responsibility. These journeys fuelled the girls' sense of global citizenship. They returned with a new-found appreciation for diversity and a burning desire to contribute to a more equitable world. Their presentations at international forums, showcasing their solutions to local challenges, garnered worldwide attention, proving that even voices from a small Zimbabwean school could resonate on the global stage.

THE LEGACY LIVES ON

As Goodhope Primary students ventured into the world, they carried with them more than just knowledge and skills. They carried the torch of Ms Taranja's legacy of empowerment, leadership and social responsibility. They were no longer just girls from Harare but agents of change, ready to leave their mark on the world.

Many graduates returned to their communities, applying their education to tackle local challenges. A small group of engineers led by Tapiwa developed a micro-grid system that brought solar power to a remote village, transforming lives with the flick of a switch. Inspired by Ms Taranja's community initiatives, another group established a youth mentorship program, sharing their knowledge and experiences with younger generations.

The ripple effect of Ms Taranja's vision continued to spread. Mothers empowered by literacy and micro-enterprises became advocates for girls' education in their communities. Inspired by the school's success, local leaders began implementing similar initiatives in other schools. Goodhope became a beacon of hope, showcasing the transformative power of education and leaving an indelible mark on the landscape of Harare.

BEYOND THE BAOBABS: A LEGACY OF COURAGE FOR GIRLS WHO DARE

As the sun dips below the baobab trees, casting long shadows across the playground, a hush falls over Goodhope Primary. Yet, the silence is not one of quiet submission, but a pregnant pause filled with the buzzing hum of a thousand unfurling dreams. In each girl's eyes, reflected in the embers of the setting sun, flickers a spark ignited by Ms Taranja, a relentless flame fuelled by the audacity to dream beyond the boundaries of what is expected.

Across the globe, countless Ms Taranjas exist, women who refuse to let societal walls stifle the symphony of possibilities within girls. Malala Yousafzai's defiant voice echoing from Swat Valley reminds us that education is a weapon against ignorance, a passport to unimaginable heights. With her unyielding spirit and unrivalled power, Serena Williams shattered glass ceilings on the tennis court, paving the way for future generations of champions to break free.

These women are not distant stars but constellations guiding our paths. Their stories whispered in classrooms and resonating in boardrooms remind us that resilience is not just a word but a muscle honed through hardship. We see it in Wangari Maathai, whose emerald legacy of trees stands as a monument to unwavering environmental activism. These are not mere names in history books; they are whispers in the wind, conveying that change is not a privilege but a responsibility. As the sun sets on another day at Goodhope, the girls gather their dreams, not as fragile wisps but as blazing torches, for Ms Taranja has taught them that dreaming is not a luxury but a necessity, a weapon against complacency, a brushstroke on the canvas of a better tomorrow.

CONCLUSION: ECHOES OF DREAMS BEYOND BAOBABS

The story of Goodhope Primary School is not just about educating young girls; it is about the power of belief, the impact of a visionary leader and the transformative potential of education. Ms Taranja's unwavering faith in her students, coupled with her innovative approach to learning, birthed a generation of empowered young women who dared to dream big and strive for a more just and equitable world. Her legacy is not one etched in stone or enshrined in a museum. It is a living pulse, a testament to the transformative power of a single spark. For each girl who dared to dream beyond the baobabs, a thousand more are inspired to ignite their flames, burning not with self-preservation but with the unwavering desire to illuminate the world around them.

So, girls, let your dreams take flight, soar beyond the baobabs, and paint the world with your brilliance. There are Ms Taranjas in your lives and your communities, women who will hold your hand and fan the flames of your ambition. Lean on their stories, draw strength from their resilience, and let their courage be your compass. Remember, the world needs your voice, vision and dreams. Dare to paint beyond the lines, beyond expectations, beyond the horizon. For within you lies the power to change your life and the world itself. Go forth, dreamers, and leave your mark on the universe.

Remember, Goodhope's story is not a distant epic but a blueprint for action. Look around your community. Is there a girl yearning for the wings of education? A mother struggling to navigate the maze of opportunity? A family longing for a beacon of hope? Be the answer to their silent pleas.

Let the echoes of Goodhope carry far and wide, a testament to the boundless potential that lies within every girl who dares to dream. This is not the end of a story but the beginning of a symphony, a chorus of voices rising from the heart of Africa, poised to paint a future where baobabs reach not for the heavens alone but for the hands of girls reaching back, ready to shape a world worthy of their dreams.

Start today. Dream big. Be the change!

Dr Patricia Gonde is not just an educator; she is a radiant beacon of hope and opportunity in the Zimbabwean education landscape. Born and raised in Mhondoro, Mashonaland East, Zimbabwe, her journey has been one of remarkable resilience and unwavering commitment to empowering future generations. Despite facing economic and societal hurdles during her early years, which led her to attend multiple schools, Dr Gonde has risen to become an international award-winning educationist, author and global speaker.

Her path is a testament to the transformative power of education. Dr Gonde's current role as head of Academics at Lusitania Primary School in Harare showcases her dedication to implementing innovative pedagogical practices and integrating technology into the learning process. As an author of two books and co-author of two internationally available titles on Amazon, her passion for knowledge extends beyond the classroom walls.

But Dr Gonde's impact transcends mere academic achievements. Her voice has resonated across borders, earning her over a hundred global awards in education and the humanitarian sector. A firm believer in women's empowerment, she champions the rights of girls and young women, encouraging them to stand tall for justice and equality.

This commitment is reflected in her roles as a board member of Imani4All and a global advisory member of Emerald EduConcept.

Dr Gonde's influence extends beyond her local community, as she represents Zimbabwe on various international platforms as an ambassador, and as Yes You Can International UK ambassador. Her research articles and her expertise as a Microsoft MIEE expert further solidify her position as a thought leader in the field of education technology.

The COVID-19 pandemic brought about a turning point in Dr Gonde's journey.

Collaborating with educators worldwide to enhance online learning during lockdown, she discovered a new-found passion for game-based learning and other e-tech tools.

This unwavering ability to adapt and embrace new technologies embodies her belief in continuous learning and growth, captured in her inspiring mantra: 'A candle loses nothing by lighting others.'

Dr Gonde's faith plays a significant role in her work. As a proud Christian, she recognises the importance of moral and emotional support for students, especially in today's increasingly complex world. Her dedication to nurturing the whole child shines through in her interactions with students, colleagues and communities.

Dr Patricia Gonde's story is not just one of personal success; it is a testament to the transformative power of education and the unwavering spirit of a woman who refused to let challenges dim her light. Her journey continues to inspire and illuminate the path for others, proving that even the most challenging circumstances can become stepping stones to greatness.

IDENTITY, MUSIC & SELF-CARE

Rebecca Rylands

OUR POTENTIAL TO MAKE A DIFFERENCE

I am a woman making a difference, and I wake up with the potential to make a difference every day. More often than not throughout my career, I've chosen to do things that help others. My capacity to support others evolves to match incoming stressors, changing seasons and roles, but ultimately, prioritising my own wellbeing today helps my future self and my loved ones. This is the greatest lesson I've learned working as a helping professional – self-care is an essential requirement.

Professionally, I've been a music teacher, counsellor, music therapist and lecturer. Personally, I've known the heartaches that come with love and loss. I've moved from New Zealand to Australia and birthed three children. I've attempted to find a work-life balance and learned to roll with change. I value bravery over striving for perfection – if I'd waited for perfect conditions before taking off, I'd still be on the runway.

Discovering where and how I would make a difference took a while. I would ask myself, *What can I do?* and in times of doubt and exhaustion, the simple answer has been, *Do what I can.* I've become more aware of my strengths and limitations, and by acknowledging and working with them, I can grow compassion for myself and others. I try to read my energy levels, reduce energy-zapping tasks where possible and choose the right jobs at the right times throughout the day. I make conscious decisions to pursue passions that inspire me and offer encouragement, hope and ideas that work for me; an imperfect person doing her best.

THE PATHS OF MUSIC AND COUNSELLING

I've often been curious about social development and activities that help create community. I've worked in schools where bullying and social anxieties were common in the therapy room. Our need to belong is so deep within us that, at times, we can avoid living fully, afraid of what others might think of us. Still, we risk failure and loss, called to continue to love and trust.

The saying *we are made stronger by being tempered in fire*, resonates with me. I have walked knowingly – and unknowingly – into risky situations. Some developed good outcomes. From others, I have walked away with a heavy heart when things didn't go as I'd hoped. Moments of failure have taught me to pivot, growing my capacity and revealing the biggest lessons of my life.

There I was, a stubborn twenty-four-year-old, straight out of teachers' college and running a music program at a large urban high school. It was a good job. I wasn't exactly sure how I'd gotten it, but I was determined to do my best by the students. I wanted to stay for at least two years so I could gain my registration. After two years, I then planned to stay for five, because I wanted to leave the department's resources and culture in a better state than how I'd found it.

I had success as a teacher but struggled to feel capable of this posting. I continued anyway, growing my skills and sharing my gifts in a job that was rewarding, though stressful. I experienced the tension between the desire to make a meaningful difference to up to thirty students in each class and how to look after myself.

Sometimes, I felt my efforts paid off. Other times, the volume of others' needs was overwhelming. To continue to work with young people and make them feel better about themselves, their lives and their futures, I undertook master's level qualifications and a counselling training program.

From my experience volunteering at a helpline service that offered free support to young people, I discovered I had the uncanny skill of staying calm in the face of a crisis, so I pursued two years of part-time study on top of my full-time teacher load.

My weekends were overtaken by study. I dug deep, making sacrifices to get things done and teetered on the verge of burnout. I pushed on through, waiting for school holidays to arrive.

In my second year of part-time study, I successfully applied for a scholarship to dedicate a year to study and complete my placement hours. My master's portfolio required a research project, so I committed to what had the most relevance and truth for me after five years as a music teacher.

CAREER TRANSITION TO A THERAPIST

For eons, people from every corner of the earth have used music and ceremony to move through life's transitions. Music can make people feel good, safe, happy, heard and seen. For my research, I applied an evidence-based approach to group music-making with teenagers.

When I discovered the use of drum circles, combined with group therapy, I headed to Australia to train in a program widespread throughout the school system there. I returned to New Zealand and got funding for twelve drums, learning how to facilitate drum therapy groups. With the group therapy facilitation skills gained through the helpline, I could provide a space that was engaging, smoother, light and, at times, profoundly deep.

After my first pilot group was complete, I started my research group. I finished my master's with first-class honours and discovered I had a gift for working therapeutically with people in smaller groups.

Despite the awards I received academically in high school, I did not feel very smart then and tried so hard to achieve success. Over time, I learned that effort can play a bigger role than talent, as a predetermining factor for success.

A year later, my Australian husband and I moved to his hometown and the next part of my journey began. I took my first job as a school counsellor in Brisbane. From there, I built my reputation and skills in schools and adult mental health settings, until I was ready to branch out with a business of my own.

MUSIC THERAPY AND MENTAL HEALTH

Initially, creating a business from what I love was slow, but then, I found myself working simultaneous gigs for as many hours as a full-time employee. After a little while, I realised I needed to be more discerning about what I took on and look out for myself.

Among conflicting pressures, I'm a little bit easier on myself these days. Thankfully, I've discovered new opportunities through the drumming program that trained me, including facilitating accredited workshops for practitioners who also want to become facilitators to use the approach with their clients.

This work has given me a couple of experiences that demonstrate the profound difference music can make. I enter aged-care facilities regularly now to run music therapy sessions, and the most interesting space for me is in the dementia unit. Nervous the first time I went in, I wondered if I had the skills, however, I noticed that the staff members were delighted to see the residents engaged in this activity and enjoying a moment together. For some participants, I saw their memories taking them back to a moment in their youth.

Music has such power. It's embedded deep in the brain where we make memories associated with feelings. Participating in music-making experiences is a whole-brain activity. We look at what people around us are doing. We hear what they're doing and respond to it. We live in the moment, on the spot. And sometimes … mistakes happen.

Occasionally, I've witnessed participants experience anxiety as they drum for the first time. Some come with previous experiences that make them feel insecure about their musical skills. Others identify as musically experienced with other instruments and may have difficulty letting go, becoming learners again. When I present rhythm-based exercises, people commonly express fear that they might do the exercise incorrectly. To build capacity in new growth areas, we need to feel the fear, stay with it for a moment to acknowledge if there is actual danger or not, and normalise the sensation of anxiety as a helpful part of the brain's warning system. Like a security alarm protecting a car, sometimes the alarm is set off by something. Until we're able to assess the situation, we remain on high alert to danger. Once the level of threat is determined, we can respond appropriately.

If we don't push past the fear and experience new things, our world can atrophy. I support people as they ride the wave of anxiety and come out the other side, looking exhilarated after trying drumming in a supportive group setting. I get consistent feedback at the end of workshops that the drumming was highly enjoyable; they had fun! Dopamine is released, and it doesn't matter if they didn't get it 'right' because we can learn and try again. The beauty of using music as a metaphor for life is that it's a safe way to explore perfectionism, performance anxiety and concepts of social support.

NEURODIVERSITY AND DRUMMING FOR RELAXATION

I used to think I needed to be perfect as a musician and wondered if I'd ever get there. I practised bass guitar eight hours a day, trying to be the best bass player I could in rock bands in my early twenties. I could never attain that perfection, although there are perfect moments in music.

Music is always moving and changing, just like we humans are always in transition. When we appreciate that moment, when we hear a sound start, we also know it begins to fade away.

A little bit like life.

The neurodiversity community is another community profoundly impacted by music therapy, and I feel I have personal insight here. Over time, I've realised that my brain works differently, and I'm okay with myself, quirks and all, but when I've explored ADHD and executive function, I see some of my personal struggles. Such revelations are less heavy and less stigmatised than they were when I was growing up.

My journey gives me a greater capacity to understand and connect with individuals who have similar experiences. Perhaps I work with someone who struggles to be on time. Perhaps it's having all their paperwork done or just getting themselves organised with their clothes folded and put away. At my house, my clothes are not always folded and put away either, but I have strengths in other areas.

Once, I was working with a group of eleven to thirteen-year-old girl students who identified as neurodivergent. Girls are often less likely to be diagnosed with ADHD and are considered better at masking it. Through the group drumming experience, some of the participants expressed how they were able to experience relaxation, and that they could be themselves without feeling judged. They were playful without getting into trouble.

Even at this young age, these girls felt the world's pressures to perform, to be perfect, to do well academically and to be liked. But after they drummed together, they experienced a sense of safety and connection. Within that setting, the drumming equalises things that may have felt disparate. Different backgrounds, and all the unknowns, disappear when people make music together. Music adds to a group's cohesiveness and sticks communities together like glue.

Throughout this experience, I've gone from assessing people on how good they are at music, to accepting people wherever they are on their musical journey, and that is so much more satisfying for me. Perhaps some of them will go on to become professional musicians, but that's not my goal. I want to see people enjoying making music in the moment, safely being themselves, dropping masks and being accepted. It's my pleasure and privilege to witness such dramatic shifts in a short time during a therapeutic drumming session.

PREGNANCY AND PROFESSIONAL GROWTH

At a point in my career when I had gained peer recognition, I travelled overseas and trained several new facilitators. At thirty weeks pregnant, I felt fit, healthy and capable of delivering such a session. I had spoken with the developer of the program about my pregnancy, and he said he wanted to move the date forward a few weeks for peace of mind. Drumming is known to kickstart labour, and he wanted to mitigate that risk. While away, I spoke with my children and husband nightly by phone and read my daughter a chapter of a book she had chosen until she fell asleep. Trying to be available for my family while holding space for others to learn and heal was exhausting. Still, keeping some of our family routines alive was necessary, even when I was out of the country.

Balance is a changing affair, and as my children grow up, they will no longer request bedtime reading and my work commitments will shift. The flexibility to pivot within my career and acclimatise to changes has been critical for my success.

CONCLUSION

Throughout the challenges, I am still here. I naturally find it easier to do things for others which could be seen as altruistic, but it also grows my self-worth when my work is appreciated. Being a born helper can be a blessing but can also lead to burnout when we have difficulties in valuing our own needs. I have learned that if there is an imbalance between giving and receiving, we can experience overwhelm and emotional reactivity. Drumming, like many creative and expressive therapies, helps me to regulate my emotions. Experiencing a relaxed state, regularly counteracts the tension, stress and the anxieties of modern life.

By following my passions, I am the real me in my all my endeavours. I continue to work on my self-care and reflective practices, which are exactly that – practice, not perfect.

If I can, I would encourage you to act today. Find what makes your heart sing and be willing to do whatever that is with messy abandon. Later, you can hone your skills and package them up neatly to help others. Serve your own soul first and get ready to unleash your latent potentiality.

For me, taking the leap to share my own journey has connected me with others on similar and intersecting paths. I believe the more we share our passions, celebrate our wins and learn from our failures, the more we can lift each other up.

Hailing from the picturesque Hokitika, New Zealand, Rebecca Rylands stands as a testament to the symbiotic relationship between music and mental wellness. A credentialed registered counsellor, an educator and a graduate from The University of Auckland receiving an honours award for her master of counselling degree in 2014, Rebecca's journey has always harmonised her passion for rhythm-based music therapies with her dedication to mental health.

Tracing her roots, Rebecca embarked on her melodic journey as a bass player in vibrant rock bands. This experience segued into her profound role as a high school music teacher and subsequently propelled her into the domain of school guidance counselling. Embracing evidence-based and trauma-informed methodologies, she accentuates the transformative power of embodied learning and community music.

Her signature therapeutic drumming techniques include the use of hand drums, shakers and voice to create a sanctuary for individuals across all skill levels. With a presence spanning Australia's Eastern states and New Zealand, she amplifies the significance of drumming groups, advocating their potential to foster holistic socio-emotional growth.

Rebecca's expertise isn't just restricted to the young. Her touch heals across life's spectrum – from assisting new mothers navigating the complexities of motherhood, mentoring adolescents amidst the turbulence of teen years, to providing aged care residents with rhythm-infused therapies.

Now anchoring her life in Brisbane, Australia, alongside her cherished family, Rebecca spearheads a distinguished private counselling practice.

REBECCA RYLANDS

This venture sees her don an array of hats: from workshop facilitator, sought-after public speaker, to a revered mentor in the mental health arena. Her invaluable insights have graced platforms like the Generation Next's Mental Health Summit and The Australian Counselling Association's Annual Conference. Furthermore, as a lecturer, she's nurturing the upcoming wave of counsellors and psychotherapists.

With a Level 4 Clinical Registration with the Australian Counselling Association, Rebecca's professional journey includes impactful stints in schools in Auckland and Brisbane, and a personally insightful tenure working in refugee mental health. A stalwart trainer and mentor for Rhythm2Recovery, she extends her teachings across Queensland and New Zealand.

Rebecca's therapeutic approach is eclectic, tailoring modalities to resonate with each client's unique needs. Passionate about cross-cultural understanding, diversity and inclusion, she strives to empower individuals with coping mechanisms for life's multifaceted challenges. Above all, she treasures the foundation of trust in her relationships, enabling individuals to delve into their potential and lead lives imbued with purpose and fulfilment.

In the grand symphony of life, Rebecca Rylands is a resonant note – melding the beauty of music with the profundity of mental health to cultivate holistic healing.

Reach out to Rebecca and embark on your healing journey at rebeccarylandscounselling.com.au

THE SILENT DIFFERENCE

Dr Sarifa Alonto-Younes

Reflecting on a transformative moment in my life, moving to Australia permanently in 1998, I faced a stark reality. Job opportunities were scarce, and finding a position that matched my qualifications seemed an insurmountable challenge. Unemployment and a temporary state of stagnation made me question my capabilities, as if they had somehow become dormant. This period of unemployment left me feeling disconnected from my abilities, wondering if I could still perform tasks I once excelled at.

However, it was in that very moment of perceived disability when I discovered the resilience and untapped potential within. I reframed the narrative and turned adversity into an opportunity for self-discovery and growth. The experience became a pivotal moment of realisation. It highlighted the importance of recognising our abilities and actively connecting with them to navigate challenges. We must not let temporary setbacks disconnect us from the reservoir of talents within. Instead, let them serve as a catalyst to propel us towards our dreams, ensuring we contribute positively to society and become integral parts of the solutions we seek. Our abilities are the key to unlocking our potential for both personal fulfilment and societal impact.

When considering what it takes to be a *woman making a difference*, I'm reminded of Sheryl Sandberg's transformative journey at Facebook. It is not just a tale of corporate triumph but a testament to the boundless possibilities that lie within each of us, waiting to be unleashed. In 2008, she assumed the role of chief operating officer during a tumultuous period when Facebook was grappling with a staggering loss of $56 million USD. Undeterred by the challenges, Sheryl's strategic prowess and visionary leadership turned the tide, repositioning Facebook as a dynamic advertising platform for small business. The ensuing decade witnessed an extraordinary ascent, with the company achieving a remarkable turnover of $22.1 billion by 2018.

Yet, Sheryl's impact extends far beyond the boardroom. Her influential book, *Lean In: Women, Work, and the Will to Lead* (co-authored with Nell Scovell), served as a catalyst for a global movement, empowering women to embrace leadership roles. Through her powerful communication and unwavering advocacy, she sparked a critical conversation on gender equality which resonated far beyond the corporate realm, challenging societal norms and inspiring change.

The essence of Sheryl's story echoes a universal truth – that we all harbour the potential for greatness within us. The only true impediment to our success lies in our ability to recognise and embrace our inherent capabilities. When we disconnect from our talents, we stifle our capacity to contribute meaningfully. Dr Harbeen Arora Rai, the president and founder of the Women Economic Forum (WEF), aptly articulates this when she emphasises that disconnecting from our abilities is tantamount to disabling ourselves.

The lessons learned from Sheryl Sandberg's journey serve as an inspirational guide, urging us to embrace challenges, lead with vision and advocate for positive change. Here's a few to consider:

1. Resilience in the Face of Challenges: Sheryl faced significant challenges at Facebook, but her resilience and ability to navigate adversity led to a remarkable turnaround. The lesson? To embrace challenges as opportunities for growth, and to cultivate resilience in the face of setbacks.
2. Visionary Leadership and Strategic Thinking Sheryl's visionary leadership played a pivotal role in repositioning Facebook. With a positive goal for the future , you can cultivate strategic thinking, embrace innovation and lead with a vision that transcends immediate

obstacles.

3. Beyond Corporate Success: Sheryl's impact extended beyond financial success to influencing societal change. It depicts that personal success should not be limited to individual achievements but can also contribute positively to the broader community to address societal issues.

4. Empowerment and Advocacy: Sheryl's book, *Lean In*, sparked a global movement for women's empowerment. Individuals can use platforms to advocate for positive change, challenging societal norms and promoting equality and empowerment.

5. Recognising and Connecting with Abilities: The story emphasises the importance of recognising and actively connecting with our abilities. It teaches us not to underestimate our potential and to actively seek opportunities to utilise our talents, even in challenging circumstances.

6. Turning Setbacks into Opportunities: Setbacks can be transformative moments, providing opportunities for self-discovery and growth, leading to a reassessment of personal and professional goals.

7. Contributing to the Greater Good: Sheryl's narrative highlights the significance of contributing positively to society. Strive to be a contributor rather than a burden, recognising that your abilities can be powerful tools for creating solutions and making a meaningful impact.

8. Continuous Self-Reflection and Learning: With continuous self-reflection and learning, we can assess our abilities stay adaptable in the face of change, and commit to lifelong learning to stay relevant and effective.

9. Fostering Inclusivity and Equality: Sheryl's advocacy for gender equality underscores the importance of fostering inclusivity in professional settings. The lesson is to actively work towards creating environments that embrace diversity and ensure equal opportunities for all.

10. Balancing Ambition with Personal Wellbeing: Sheryl's emphasis on

'leaning in' is also a reminder to balance professional ambitions with personal wellbeing. Remember to pursue success, while being mindful of maintaining a healthy work-life balance and overall wellbeing.

Temporary setbacks should not be viewed as permanent disconnections from your reservoir of talents but rather as opportunities to propel you toward your dreams.

When you feel your abilities slipping away or the path to success seems obscured, remember this: your abilities are not diminishing, they are evolving strengths awaiting your acknowledgment. Reconnect with them, not as relics of the past, but as dynamic forces propelling you forward.

Empower yourself by acknowledging and embracing your unique abilities. They are the powerful tools that will propel you towards your dreams and success. Never underestimate the transformative potential within you – connect with your abilities, channel them purposefully and witness the extraordinary impact they can have on your journey.

Though it is not merely about acknowledging your abilities, it's also to actively connect with them. Failing to do so deprives us of the opportunity to manifest our dreams and achieve success. Your abilities are the linchpin unlocking the door to your potential – a potential not only for personal fulfilment but also for profound societal impact. Embrace your abilities, connect with them and watch as they propel you toward a future where success and contribution converge in a harmonious symphony.

Your abilities are the engine driving your journey. Embrace them, cultivate them, and watch as they transform challenges into stepping stones. Whenever you feel disconnected from your abilities, you are on the brink of a profound reconnection, ready to harness your skills and redefine your narrative.

They are the building blocks of your resilience, the architects of your success. Recognise them, leverage them, and let them guide you towards a future where your dreams become not just aspirations but tangible realities. Your abilities are your superpower – empower yourself and embark on a journey of limitless potential.

DR SARIFA ALONTO-YOUNES

Dr Sarifa Alonto-Younes is a multiple-award-winning International Speaker, Serial Edupreneur, Bestselling Author and a Philanthropist.

Sarifa is the President and Founder of the International Academy of Marawi (I AM), Philippines; Director and Co-Founder of Training College of Australia; CEO and Founder of Arndell Park Early Childhood Learning Centre; Global Director of Speakers Tribe Women, Australia and Australia Country Chair on Business Networking under the auspices of ALL Ladies League.

Sarifa holds a Bachelor of Science in Psychology, Master's Degree in Industrial and Organizational Psychology, Master's Degree in Education & Training and Doctorate in Education.

Her education, rich leadership experiences and background made her a strong voice on the international stage. She speaks on education, organisational change, personal growth, empowerment for women, leadership and management. She resides in Melbourne, Australia with her husband, Hassan, and her four children.

As a leader of leaders and a giver to givers, she is admired for her ability to listen to and support those in need. Sarifa has a passion for education and a love for humanity, and dreams of a world where young girls and orphans are given a fighting chance at a quality life, and the ability not only to survive scarcity, but to be able to savour in the gifts and rewards education can provide.

Her achievements have earned her multiple awards, locally and globally: a recipient of Australia 2018 AusMumpreneur Multicultural

DR SARIFA ALONTO-YOUNES

Business Excellence Award; 2020 Mother Theresa Award, WOHA United Kingdom; 2021 Philanthropy Award, World Women Vision Awards; a WAW Honorary Award Hall of Fame and Honorary life member of ALL Ladies League; Australia Country Chair for Business Networking under the auspices ALL Ladies League.

Her number one bestselling book, *Love Your Obstacles*, received a Bronze Medal Award at Golden Door-REX Karmaveer Truth-Writer Fellowship & Chakra Awards, which is instituted by iCongo and in partnership with United Nations. Also an Honorary mention at Golden Door 2021- Truth & Integrity of the Written Word.

Sarifa is also a co-author of six number-one bestselling books and is co-authoring few more, with another book on women's leadership about to be published. She has published fifty-to articles and still counting.

Moreover, Sarifa is now in the process of expanding her existing orphanage program by establishing a comprehensive orphanage facility for orphaned girls in the Philippines.

Website: sarifayounes.com

EMPOWER TO FEEL EMPOWERED

Zara Celik

I vividly remember when I had the open invitation to contribute to this book; I knew immediately it was going to be dedicated to my grandmother, my mother and all the strong, resilient women I have met throughout my life journey. I envisioned the content of my chapter and felt an incredible joy, empowerment and energy. This was definitely a *calling*. I happily accepted the invitation to become a contributing author, to share some of my life story and the difference women have made in my life journey with their contributions.

I'm extremely grateful for the opportunity to contribute, as I get to share my gratitude and appreciation to those women who contributed to my life, and roles they played in making a difference in my life.

My intention was to pen this chapter during the European summer of 2023, within the confines of my childhood home in Turkey. Nestled in the breathtaking, 360-degree hilltop panorama, the view spans over the valley with the crisp blue waters of the Munzur River flowing through, encompassed by towering mountains. This locale holds particular significance, as it represents the landscape where I spent the initial fourteen years of my life. However, this was not accomplished due to the sudden passing of loved ones, including my grandmother, who passed away at the age of 110 in July 2023.

I eagerly looked forward to sitting beneath the ancient mulberry and walnut trees, which my grandmother had planted, enjoying the smell of the walnut leaves in the breeze. I wanted to look out at the amazing view of the valley, whilst reflecting on the significant impact of the women who shaped my life as a young child. I would sit under those trees, up until the age of fourteen, dreaming of my future goals, analysing the shapes of the clouds and counting the stars in the night sky. In more recent times, when I go there, I have beautiful childhood memories of joy, happiness and laughter.

Until the age of fourteen, I lived with my grandmother, Haskar. She was both my mother and grandmother. I had the privilege of sharing a final moment with her, receiving her blessing and witnessing her beautiful smile, as I kissed her hand. Her resilience, wisdom and forward thinking, particularly in the realms of reproduction and creation, have always been a source of admiration.

My grandmother has been the biggest influence, mentor, teacher and source of inspiration for the lifestyle I have now and my career today. Her wisdom in wild greens, herbs and their healing properties was astonishing. She ate wild, seasonal, local, beyond organic and crafted her own simple natural skin and hair care products. She grew the wheat and lentils according to the moon calendar and cycle to cultivate seeds and grains, while using the sun for picking vegetables. Both my mother and grandmother followed regenerative farming, intuitively, having respect for the soil and its regeneration. They made their butter and cheese at home. They used stone mills to make flour and bread. They had so much love and respect towards animals; all the sheep, goats and cows had names and would come when their name was called. There was much wisdom, experience and knowledge, which I got to see, experience and practice.

I would love to take this opportunity to give respect and gratitude to my grandmother and mother. They significantly contributed to my life journey, helping me to create the trajectory of my life based on my desired goals to serve in health and wellness. They have been the greatest teachers, mentors, influencers and a source of inspiration. My mother valued education as she was not able to go to school. This was embedded in my nervous system, and I appreciate it so very much. Even now, I continue to study and learn something new every year. This has supported me to gain knowledge in different areas of life and experience. I somehow bring that to my management in health and wellness. The contribution and influence of both my mother and grandmother helped me to be the person I am today. They loved and nurtured me with an open heart. They supported me to have a strong foundation. I would like to also give my gratitude and appreciation to all the other women who have contributed to my life and growth through education, friendship, business and my career journey. I am equally grateful for the support … and the challenges. They helped me to have confidence, expand my horizon, my knowledge, professional development and experience. Women have supported and challenged me in my business life, which has accelerated my growth, personal development and recognition, as well as contributing to my financial independence.

The best way to make a difference, and to continue making difference, as well as being able to sustain that in life, is to invest and empower self in all areas of life. To achieve this, we must get the human-self to connect with source. Take care of the mind, body and soul, so that the source (spirit) unites with the human-self. Lack of daily investment creates imbalance, and over time, the human-self becomes distant or detached from the source-self. Self-empowerment is where mind and body align and work in synchronicity without interference, ensuring the soul is well-fed to connect with spirit. Empowerment enables us to make a remarkable difference within our self, and in our children, by enabling a stable and strong foundation for our family, community and people around the globe. Self-empowerment enables authenticity, a clear perspective on our mission and contribution to people in our life journey. Empowerment enables us to connect with our roots.

Empower yourself in eight areas of life to make a difference in self and in others

ENABLING A STRONG FOUNDATION

A strong and reliable foundation creates stability, balance, growth, self-belief, self-love and abundance. Just like those high-rise buildings, if they don't have strong foundations, they won't be able to support the entire building. They won't be able to resist strong winds, earthquakes and floods. They will shake and collapse with any force.

Upon reflecting and looking back on my childhood years, I appreciate the contribution of women (primarily my mother and grandmother) to my strong foundation. I was surrounded by strong women who showed and displayed discipline, commitment, consistency and perseverance.

This prepared me for innovation, success, abundance and fulfilment in all areas of my life. The most important factors were unconditional love, care, compassion, support and the challenge to be strong and independent. I was given opportunities to gain life skills with consistent daily practice, so I was equipped to be self-sufficient and independent. I was encouraged to problem-solve and overcome challenges on my own, to prepare myself for a growth mindset and leadership.

It's so important to hold space and help youth create and have stable foundation, so they too are resilient to any wind, turbulence, conflict and other predictable and non-predictable natural challenges thrown at them. Allow them to analyse challenges, remain objective, develop problem-solving strategies and self-governance. Practising in the early years of life is advantageous, however practice at any stage of life makes progress and contributes to a strong foundation which will make a significant difference in life. I say this from my personal experience, working with people in a clinical practice and mentoring people at a global level.

I loved that my mother and grandmother demonstrated self-love and self-respect.

Loving self was shown to me, primarily by actions and not so much in words. Actions definitely speak louder and clearer than words. Visual input is a more powerful memory than auditory; it's easier to forget what we heard than what we consistently see. I truly appreciate those women in my circle, during my early years of life, for not commenting or discussing their physical appearance, weight or shape. I appreciate that they didn't compare themselves to anyone and just loved themselves and others for being who they are, appreciating one another.

There was no discussion of people of colour, religion or war. This is something I now share with people in my circle, as growing up, there was no stored or biased content in my subconscious brain. My grandmother made sure she never discussed the war traumas and would not allow any of her friends to share or discuss their past traumas, abuse or phobias. I am deeply grateful as there was no reference in my brain, until I personally witnessed trauma. It's important to remember that all the information we hear and see gets stored in our brain, contributing to our foundation.

I remember my grandmother, mother and grandfather waking before sunrise to greet the sun. This was their daily gratitude practice. I find I do the same spontaneously, as it was anchored into my nervous system through repetitive visual input.

PERSONAL GROWTH AND DEVELOPMENT

VALUE AND EMPOWER YOURSELF AND GAIN CLARITY ON SELF-IDENTITY

I believe the best investments in life are health and personal development. I mentioned that prioritising and investing in health, with discipline, is naturally empowering and increases our self-worth and self-love.

Personal development helps to support us with self-awareness, self-identity and self-esteem. It helps with confidence and self-governance. Personal development supports us in the area of communication, enabling us to be congruent and articulate. Personal development helps with learning and knowledge about self, which then adds value to gaining better interpersonal skills and resilience. It is an investment to gain skills and to have better relationships with people in our personal and professional environment.

Personal development gives us insight into understanding human behaviour and psychology, which is relatable, helping us to be objective and have self-governance. We naturally become more understanding and let go of resentment, judgement and dysmorphia. We realise and appreciate loving ourselves for who we are, while appreciating others for being who they are. It creates peace, equilibrium, homeostasis and balance within, enabling equity between self and others. This calms and brings balance to the nervous system, particularly the sympathetic branch of the autonomic nervous system.

People appreciate calm, articulate and congruent people, as they feel inspired and empowered in their presence. This is an incredible way to make a difference, bringing out the true leader within.

Attending personal development courses and having a personal development coach is the best way to accelerate learning and skill in this area of life. Personal development has helped me tremendously and brought opportunities and invitations into my life as I manifested.

EMPOWER YOUR MENTAL HEALTH

Empower your mental health by having reflective awareness, being objective and appreciating that things happen for us, not to us, and that it's all on the way – not in the way. Reflective awareness means analysing objectively, being fully aware and mindful. When we have reflective awareness, we tend to operate and lead from our prefrontal cortex. This is the desired state for mental health and wellness, as this is where we get to be objective, creative, innovative and demonstrate leadership. In this state, we don't judge or criticise self or others. The nervous system will be balanced, and we won't be in fight-or-flight response. Our self-worth increases and we will be more productive, energised, fulfilled, happy, committed, self-governed and empowered.

The question then becomes, *how can we enable the activity of the prefrontal cortex and have reflective awareness?*

Get to know high-priority values in your life. Don't let the values of society rule, dictate and determine your values for you. Discover what is really important and a priority in your life. This will help you to be authentic and not compare yourself to others, their goals, dreams and achievements. Having clarity on your values and full awareness of your perception allows you to see both sides of anything occurring in life, objectively seeing both the positives and negatives, advantages and disadvantages.

Be conscious of perceptions. Perceptions determine our thoughts, decisions and actions. Our values contribute to our perceptions. Our perceptions lead to meaning, meaning leads to language and the words that we use. To describe the perceived information creates cellular energy which determines our feelings and our actions or reactions.

Let go of resentment and infatuations. The actions and traits we perceive and resent in others, in fact, exist within us. However, we may be unaware or feel embarrassed to admit to it. Infatuation is when we look up and admire others, not realising that what we see and admire in them are the traits and actions we also have, and perhaps we're too humble to admit that we display those traits. Resentments and infatuations create dis-equilibrium in the brain biochemistry by increasing activity in the amygdala – the part of the brain which responds to distress. Owning traits and actions that we resent or admire in others will bring balance to brain biochemistry. This will increase the activity in the prefrontal cortex and calm the amygdala, allowing us to have reflective awareness and balanced perceptions.

Let go of dysmorphia. When we compare our life achievements, career, finances, relationship, business, physical fitness or mental fitness to other people we know or follow on social media, we will bring imbalance to the brain biochemistry by activating amygdala response. This is self-deprecating and devaluing. Instead, see your growth and set realistic, measurable goals that are fully aligned and congruent with your values.

Invest in having a healthy gut microbiome lifestyle by following a bio-individual specific diet, meditation and exercise to help promote healthy levels of dopamine, serotonin, endorphins and oxytocin. These are the hormones in the brain called neurotransmitters and promote happiness and pleasure. A state of mental happiness will be visible in the physical body and vice versa.

Mental health and physical health are interlinked and work synchronously. Internal cellular stress (which comes in different forms) inflicted by our perceptions allows the nervous system to become imbalanced. The brain biochemistry also becomes imbalanced, the amygdala response more activated, the body goes into fight-or-flight, the parasympathetic nervous system becomes down-regulated, gut health function decreases, while heartbeat and breathing changes. When we are happy, our chest is open, our shoulders back, with upright posture and relaxed facial muscles. When we are sad, the opposite applies – shoulders become rounded, we slouch, head looking down.

Having self-awareness and self-governance is the output of a well-equilibrated mind. This is where we are intuitive, authentic and feel empowered. People appreciate this and are drawn to authenticity like a magnet.

EMPOWER PHYSICAL HEALTH

Empowering self to have vitality allows us to thrive geometrically in all areas our lives, as the human self will be in a state of equilibrium and homeostasis. Being and feeling physically healthy, fit and energetic contributes to mental health and wellbeing. A well-synchronised mind-body communication is a state of equanimity, balance and homeostasis.

Aim to have consistency and discipline when it comes to investing in yourself in the area of physical health. We all love and appreciate a state of balance. Cells in our body also want a state of balance, equilibrium and homeostasis. At an optimal functional state, all cells communicate and contribute to cellular health, proactively and productively. When cells work together as a team, with no distraction or disturbance, they are fully energetic, vibrant and happy. They will heal within and that will translate to us being at optimal health and feeling energetic and empowered.

Feeling empowered through the discipline of self-care will allow us to perform at a peak energetic state. And this is where we are innovative, creative, objective, playful, joyful and at balance. This is the state of having desire and commitment to contribute and serve others to make a difference.

Cells in our body are energetic and communicate via energy. When there is any interference, disturbance or interruption to the cellular energy, this creates a state of *dis-ease*. We can all agree that when we have a headache, or any pain or discomfort, it affects our presence, state of energy, concentration, psychology, emotional health, mental health, relationships, communication and the function of our autonomic nervous system and vagus nerve. Optimum cellular function equates to optimal state of physical, mental, emotional, psychological health and wellness.

In the case of chronic illness, pain, inflammation and serious health issues, the impact of disturbance in the cellular energies will be more significant. Unfortunately, with an unwell and non-optimal state of health, no-one will feel empowered. This hinders our ability to serve ourselves and others, and we will not be able to make a difference or have the impact we would like to make.

Invest in physical health and wellness consistently, every day, by drinking enough water, movement, stretching, time in nature, sweating in steam rooms, as well as exercising and eating foods that serve your bio individuality. Minimising or eliminating stimulants, such as caffeine and sugar, getting enough sleep and getting support from allied health professionals, such as a chiropractor, acupuncture and massage, will assist in your physical health.

EMPOWER THE SOUL

People in society mainly talk about and focus on the importance of mental and physical health. If we want our human-self to be functioning at an optimal state, we must also factor in what feeds the soul. When we lack what feeds the soul and only focus on the health of the mind and physical health, we miss the most critical element of the puzzle that contributes to our health, wellbeing and vitality. This is where the human-self becomes distant from the source-self. Investing and feeding the soul is one of the primary foods. Deficiency in primary foods will stop us from feeling energised and empowered. The most important primary food that feeds the soul is the relationships we have with people in our life, including our loved ones, intimate partner and people in our circle. We could have all the money, success, business, career and education in the world, but when we have tension with a loved one, we won't be happy. It is important we invest in building healthy relationships with people in our circle to nourish and to thrive in life.

EMPOWER YOURSELF IN THE AREA OF FINANCIAL SUCCESS

Having financial success gives us freedom, choice, confidence, prosperity, power, as well as proximity to those in power and a chance to contribute to others financially.

In my life journey, I have learned that money is an energetic game. To create financial success an individual must have a clear goal and it must be high value. One must demonstrate that wealth building is a high value by saving, investing and avoiding spending for immediate gratification. Financial income has a thermostat. When we say we will make 'X dollars' we will in fact make that 'X dollar'. This is like setting the thermostat in a house to a certain temperature. Once it hits that temperature, it will stop and once it goes down, it will work towards the set temperature again.

Many of us in business might agree that when we don't feel like going to work one day – clients cancel. But when we go in with a high-vibrational energetic state, stay present and show interest to help others – money and business flourish. This is because money is an energetic game, and we must serve to be rewarded with money as fair exchange.

I don't believe anyone can make money with no effort or a desire to create and have financial success. There must be a purpose behind financial success, and one must serve from the heart and contribute to making a difference in the world and in the life of others, so that the universe can reward in fair exchange with financial wealth gain.

Money creates power. We live in a world and society that when we have financial wealth, we are perceived as rich. Most of the financially wealthy people I work with have proximity to powerful people in the world, such as politicians and world leaders. Their schedule consists of making connections and networking with those people in power. They are invited to events. They are given speaking opportunities. They run high-ticket events, create and form a community of people who have wealth building as one of their high values. So, it's win-win and based on fair exchange. They serve like-minded people, make an impact, make a difference, form a community, feel powerful, feel empowered, feel fulfilled and get handsomely paid for making that difference by service.

They empower themselves and the people they serve. People are magnetically drawn to them, and they make a huge difference through power of financial freedom and wealth. That's why I believe it's important that we empower ourselves to have financial success and freedom, to make a difference and contribute to others, by supporting disadvantaged people in our communities and around the world and having proximity to those in power to make a difference.

SOCIAL EMPOWERMENT

Proximity truly is power. Surround yourself with people who are inspiring and dedicated to their mission, playing their game at a higher level. Get to know people, network, choose to empower and elevate them and have intention to build connection, trust and relationships. Be true and authentic without the facade, as a facade is exhausting, and as people connect with each other via an energy exchange, they will feel when you are not authentic. Authenticity is magnetic.

Being authentic means that we love and appreciate who we are, as we are. Owning and appreciating our own bio-individual identity is extremely powerful and impactful on its own. It is attractive, as people are energetic and spiritual beings. People appreciate and love to surround themselves with high-vibrational energy. This high frequency of vibrational energy exists in those people who are enlightened, well invested, have full reflective awareness and know their own identity, carrying that badge of self-identity with pride and honour. And those people empower others significantly.

EMPOWER SPIRITUALLY

Spiritual empowerment, in my opinion, is when the human-self has a state of equanimity, homeostasis and balance within. When the human self has equanimity, the energy flow in the cells and within the cells has no interference, disturbances or dissipation. Energised cells mean happy humans, and a happy human is well invested. A well-invested person has reflective awareness, no judgement, full gratitude, loves self and has appreciation of self and others. This is where the human-self is united with source. This is a state of enlightenment, and an enlightened person is spiritually empowered.

Making a difference in someone is the greatest gift one can cherish, as the gratitude and blessing of that is very rewarding. Be generous to share your wisdom and knowledge, as you never know when one word you use will make a difference in another's life journey. To be able to make an impact and empower someone, it is important we invest in ourselves, so we are empowered. Invest in physical health, mental health, feed the soul to connect with source to have balance, equanimity and thrive in all areas of life. Invest in personal development and choose to be your authentic self and serve from the heart.

Dr Zara Celik is an integrative health and nutrition practitioner, wellness expert and high-performance mindset mentor who is dedicated to intuitively transforming lives and empowering people to connect with source, have abundant energy and vitality to thrive geometrically in all areas of their lives.

Dr Zara is committed to educating, supporting, guiding people to connect with inner-self, understand and expand their knowledge, awareness and gain wisdom about their mental, emotional, physical and spiritual wellbeing and teach them how to be able to create equanimity and sustainable homeostasis within.

Dr Zara has been committed to inspiring and serving thousands of people around the globe including celebrities, CEOs, entrepreneurs, business owners, health care professionals and athletes.

Since the age of four, she had a clear vision of helping people as an intuitive holistic healer and her goal was to study and learn everything related to human body, brain, psychology and behaviour.

She studied bachelor of science at the University of Melbourne majoring in applied mathematics, anatomy and physiology.

Fascinated by the power of the nervous system and neuroscience, Dr Zara went on to complete a double degree in applied science and complementary medicine, chiropractic followed by masters in clinical chiropractic and masters of wellness at RMIT University.

She knew that nutrition played a significant role in the healing process to achieve optimum health and vitality and that not one particular diet serves everyone the same way, as everyone is bio-individual. Dr Zara wanted to advance her knowledge in integrative and functional nutrition to support her clients to achieve sustainable outcomes. Dr Zara has completed her studies in integrative functional nutrition health coaching at the Institute for Integrative Nutrition in New York, she is a qualified health and wellness coach and has special interest in endocrine (hormone), skin and gut health nutrition, human behaviour and psychology and mindset.

Dr Zara Celik is an alchemist in human physiology and biochemistry where she uses the skin conditions and symptoms and maps it to specific organ involvement along with extensive clinical testing to find the root cause of symptoms, which took her a decade in clinical practice to master.

Dr Zara believes that everybody thrives on a diet that is specific to their microbiome which can be determined by microbiome study findings. She is the only practitioner who specialises in the 'microbiome diet' globally.

While working with private patients and clients she noticed that language pattern, condition of the mind and perceptions played a role in determining and altering the state of being and flow of energy in the physical body. With a strong desire to serve her patients and clients with excellence, Dr Zara wanted to advance her education and master balancing the mind to help her clients transcend, be authentic, creative, objective and achieve a state of poise. Dr Zara has been studying at The Demartini Institute with her mentor Dr John Demartini who is world-renowned human behaviour specialist, to gain mastery in Demartini technique to balance the mind, dissolve trauma, clear resentment, infatuation and grief to create homeostasis and state of vitality in her clients.

Dr Zara is a mother of four children and is founder and managing director of multi-award-winning Amara Wellness Centre, which recently got featured in *Global Business Leaders* magazine as one of the thirty innovative companies. Amara Wellness Centre was awarded as Best Wellness

WOMEN MAKING A DIFFERENCE

Centre in Australia, Best International Spa, Best Wellness Studio and Client Excellence Award.

Dr Zara is executive contributor of *Brainz* magazine and was finalist at AusMumpenur awards in the year 2022 and author.

THIS BOOK CHANGES LIVES

Proceeds from the sale of this book go to providing marginalised women in business with scholarships to enable them to receive support, mentoring and education through The Women's Business School.

Aligning with the United Nations SDG goals for gender equality, The Women's Business School scholarships are awarded to women in remote and rural areas, First Nations women, migrant women, survivors of domestic violence, women with disability and chronic illness and those facing financial hardship.

We believe that investing in women is the most powerful way to change the world, and these scholarships provide opportunities for deserving women to participate in an incubator program for early stage startups and businesses and an accelerator program for high-potential entrepreneurs ready to scale their companies and expand globally.

You can read more about the work of The Women's Business School Scholarship Program and how they're changing the world here:

thewomensbusinessschool.com/scholarship

ABOUT PEACE & KATY AND SPEAKING OPPORTUNITIES

Peace and Katy are the dynamic duo behind AusMumpreneur, Australia's number-one community for mums in business; The Women's Business School, providing dedicated education for aspiring and established female founders; Women Changing the World Press, amplifying the voices of thought leaders, female founders and women changing the world; and Women Changing the World Investments, providing opportunities for capital for female founders.

Peace Mitchell is a TEDx speaker, international keynote speaker, retreat facilitator and workshop presenter.

If you want your audience to be captivated by a heart-centred, warm and engaging thought leader and speaker then look no further.

With experience delivering keynote presentations on connection, business success, magic and productivity, there's nothing Peace loves more than engaging with your delegates to make your event a huge success.

If you've got an online or in-person event coming up and want to create a magical, warm and engaging atmosphere, please get in touch.

peace@womensbusinesscollective.com
+61 431 615 107

ABOUT THE WOMEN'S BUSINESS SCHOOL

The Women's Business School is a business school designed exclusively for women. Providing opportunities for innovative female founders to scale their startup, connect with fellow founders and gain advice and guidance from successful entrepreneurs and experts. Through the award-winning incubator and accelerator programs, founders receive world-class entrepreneurial education from a team of high-level experts and entrepreneurs as well as mentoring, advice and access to successful female entrepreneurs across a range of industries. If you're ready to take your business to the next level apply today!

thewomensbusinessschool.com

ABOUT AUSMUMPRENEUR

Australia's number-one community for mumpreneurs. The AusMum-preneur Awards are a national event recognising and celebrating Australia's best and brightest mums in business. Held annually, these awards recognise the incredible women who are balancing business and motherhood and creating innovative, high-quality and remarkable brands across a range of industries.

ausmumpreneur.com

ABOUT WOMEN CHANGING THE WORLD PRESS

Women Changing the World press publishes thought leaders, female founders and women who are committed to making the world a better place through their words and actions. We believe that investing in women is the most powerful way to change the world and we are passionate about amplifying women's voices, stories and ideas and providing more opportunities for women to share their message with the world. If you have a story that the world needs to hear get in touch today.

wcwpress.com

ABOUT WOMEN CHANGING THE WORLD AWARDS

The Women Changing the World Awards recognises, acknowledges and celebrates the trailblazers, changemakers and visionary action-takers. Providing a platform to amplify the achievements, accomplishments and work that women around the world are doing to make a difference in big and small ways. We believe that by elevating women, their ideas and their impact we can create a ripple effect that not only celebrates these women and the incredible work that they do but also inspires others to take action and make the world a better place in their own way too.

wcwawards.com

www.ingramcontent.com/pod-product-compliance
Lightning Source LLC
Chambersburg PA
CBHW060551080526
44585CB00013B/524